Edmund B. O'Callaghan

Voyages of the Slavers St. John and Arms of Amsterdam, 1659, 1663

Together with additional papers illustrative of the slave trade under the Dutch. Vol. 3

Edmund B. O'Callaghan

Voyages of the Slavers St. John and Arms of Amsterdam, 1659, 1663
Together with additional papers illustrative of the slave trade under the Dutch. Vol. 3

ISBN/EAN: 9783337308605

Printed in Europe, USA, Canada, Australia, Japan

Cover: Foto ©Andreas Hilbeck / pixelio.de

More available books at **www.hansebooks.com**

VOYAGES

OF THE SLAVERS

St. John and Arms of Amsterdam,

1659, 1663;

TOGETHER WITH

Additional Papers *illuſtrative of the Slave Trade under the Dutch.*

TRANSLATED FROM THE ORIGINAL MANUSCRIPTS,

WITH AN

Introduction and Index,

By E. B. O'CALLAGHAN.

ALBANY, N. Y.,
J. MUNSELL, 82 STATE ST.
1867.

No.

Edition, 100 Copies.

INTRODUCTION.

N THE Tract now publifhed, we have collected and tranflated the Papers in the Secretary of State's Office, illuftrative of Slavery and the Slave Trade under the Dutch. As the Documents are authentic, they furnifh reliable Material for a Chapter in the early Hiftory of our State at prefent unwritten, and hitherto but partially known.

To the Dutch undoubtedly belongs the queftionable Diftinction of having introduced Negro Slavery into the Colonies, now the *United States of America.* "About the laft of *Auguft*" (1619), fays *John Rolfe*, the celebrated Hufband of *Pocahontas*, writing from *Virginia*, "came in a Dutch man of warre, that fold vs twenty Negars."* *Oldmixon* refers to the fame Event, but leaves

<small>Smith's General Hiftory of Virginia, Ed. 1627, P. 126, Richmond Ed., II, 39.</small>

---

* This Event is generally ftated to have occurred in 1620; but a careful Perufal of *Smith* fhows that it took place in 1619. Mr. *Bancroft*, *Hift. U. S.*, 1ft Ed., I, 189, quotes *Beverley* as the original Authority for this Fact. *Beverley* only copied Capt. *Smith*, without acknowledging the Source of his Information; of which Circumftance Mr. *Bancroft* does not appear to have been aware.

Introduction. vii

the Impreffion that the Veffel was a Merchantman. "The Merchant fold 20 Negroes, which were the firft Slaves that were brought thither (to *Virginia*) from *Guinea*." [*Britifh Empire in America*, Ed. 1741, I, 369.]

At this Period a Clafs of Adventurers, called "*Guinea* Traders," reforted to *Africa;* another Clafs, called "*Virginia* Traders," reforted to *America*. One or other of thefe, it is fuppofed, landed the above mentioned Negroes.

In 1621, all the Dutch private Companies trading to *Africa* and *America* were merged into one— the celebrated Weft India Company—which, by Virtue of its Charter, raifed Troops, fitted out Men-of-War, and made other Preparations for entering the Field againft *Spain*. This Power had, at that time, the almoft entire Control of the Trade of *Africa*, from which Country it imported into *Brazil*, during the four Years ending 1623, *Fifteen thoufand, four hundred and thirty* Blacks, to work its Sugar Plantations.

<small>De Lact, Jaerlyk Verhael, 192.</small>

In 1623, the Weft India Company commenced Hoftilities, which it continued with confiderable Vigor for feveral Years. At firft, how-

Introduction. ix

ever, it placed no Value on the Negroes it captured from the Spaniards; for in 1624, Admiral *Van Dort* having overhauled, off the Coaſt of *Brazil*, a Spaniſh Veſſel carrying Blacks from *Angola* to *Bahia*, took the Skipper and let the Ship and Blacks go, " not knowing," frankly confeſſes *De Laet*, "how uſeful and profitable they could be to them." Again, in 1627, the Dutch having overcome a Portugueſe Ship, coming from *Angola* to *Pernambuco* with 600 Blacks on board, they derived no Advantage from the Capture, as

Jaerlyk Verhael, P. 17.

Ibid., P. 120, 121.

thofe of *Pernambuco* refufed to ranfom the Negroes, fome of whom were landed afterwards, with the Portuguefe, at *Fayal.* And fo late as 1631, two Ships from *Angola* with 850 Negroes, having been captured off *Hifpaniola* and *Sta.* *Martha,* the Dutch Commanders not knowing what to do with the Blacks, let them and the Ships go.

<small>De Laet, Ibid., P. 230, 270.</small>

It will be feen by the above *Refumé,* that the Weft India Company having been abforbed in its Operations againft the Spaniards, did not, for fome Years after it

Introduction. xi

first came into Existence, place much Value on the Slave Trade; and, as a Consequence, Slavery was not greatly fostered or encouraged in *New Netherland.*

It was not until the Dutch had reduced *Pernambuco* and other Parts of *Brazil*, and taken *Curaçao*, that they began to derive any Profit from the Capture of Slaves. In *October*, 1636, the *Soutbergh* took a Ship from *Angola* with 230 Negroes, which were sold shortly afterwards at the *Reciff* for 30,000 Guilders. A couple of Months later, another Lot of captured Afri-

De Laet, Ibid., P. 528, 529.

cans, 340 in Number, was fold by public Auction at the fame Place, and brought 67,000 Guilders. Between the Years 1623 and 1636, the Dutch captured from the Spaniards *Two thousand, three hundred and fifty-six* Negroes, whofe eftimated Value was 589,000 Guilders. Finally, in 1641, they reduced *Loando St. Paulo* in *Africa;* and thus, with this Slave Hive on the one Side, and *Brazil* and *Curaçao* for Slave Markets on the other, they obtained complete Control of the Slave Trade. The Ships of the Weft India Company now failed direct from *Holland* to

De Laet, Ibid., App. P. 21.

Southey's Brazil.

Introduction. xiii

Angola with Articles of Commerce; got Slaves in Exchange, which they carried to *Brazil,* and returned to *Holland* with Sugar and other Produce of that Country.

We now propofe to trace the Introduction of Slavery into *New Netherland.*

In 1625 or 1626, fix or feven Years after the Dutch had difcharged the fmall Lot of Slaves in *Virginia,* the firft Negroes were brought to *Manhattan.* Among them were *Paul d'Angola, Simon Congo, Anthony Portuguefe, John Francifco,* and feven other Africans, who were probably captured at Sea. Their Names denote the Country to which they originally belonged. Two Years afterwards three Negro Women arrived at *New Amſterdam;* and theſe are the only Inſtances on Record of the Introduction of Slaves in *New Netherland* prior to the Erection of Patroonſhips and Colonies in 1629, when the Weſt India Company publicly promiſed to "uſe their Endeavors to ſupply the Coloniſts with as many Blacks as they conveniently can."

<small>*Freedoms of* 1629, Art. 30.</small>

For Cauſes, already noted, theſe "endeavors" were not followed, as

Introduction. xv

far as we have been able to afcertain, by any immediate Increafe of Negroes here; and it was not until after the Reduction of *Loando* that the Current of Slavery fet northward to any great Amount.*

By an Edict iffued in 1645, no private Dutch Veffel was allowed to trade farther North than *Cape Florida*, nor on any Account to the *Virginias, New Netherland, New France*, the Coaft of *Africa* or *Brazil.* The Trade in thefe Coun-

N. Y. Colonial Doc., I, 223.

---

* Slavery exifted in the Limits of the prefent State of *New Jerfey* as early as 1638.—*N. Y. Col. MSS.*, I, 41.

tries was wholly monopolized by the West India Company.

In the Summer of 1646, the first Slave Ship, of whose Name we have a Record, arrived in *New Netherland*. She was called the *Amandaré*. This Vessel touched at *Barbadoes*, where "three Negro Wenches" were spirited away. The Remainder arrived at *New Amsterdam* in *June*, where "the Negroes were sold for Pork and Peas. Something wonderful was to be performed with them, but they just dropped through the Fingers." What Number of Slaves were brought in

Vanderdonck Vertoogh.

Introduction. xvii

this Veffel, or whether they were brought from *Brazil* or *Guinea,* is not ſtáted.*

In *January*, 1648, a Committee of the States General made a lengthy Report on the Affairs of the Weſt India Company, in the Courſe of which they refer to the Fact, that in Conſequence of the unſettled State of *Brazil,* "the Slave Trade hath long lain dormant to the great Damage of the Company." In order to revive that Traffic,

---

* Sugar and Oil were a Part of her Cargo; and theſe Articles may ſerve as a Clue to determine her Port of Departure. She undoubtedly belonged to, or was chartered by, the Weſt India Company.

Attention was turned to *New Netherland*.

N. Y. Colonial Doc., I, 246.

"That Country," says the Report, "is considered to be the most fruitful of all within your High Mightinesses' Jurisdiction, and the best adapted to raise all Sorts of this Country Produce, such as Rye, Wheat, Barley, Peas, Beans, etc., and Cattle; and that in more Abundance than can be done here, were it suitably peopled and cultivated. The granting of Freedoms and Privileges, hath indeed induced some Patroons and Colonists to undertake Agriculture there; but as the Produce cannot be fold any where except in the adjacent Places belonging to the Englifh, who are themfelves fufficiently fupplied, thofe Planters have not received a Return for their Labor and Outlay. With a View, then, to give greater Encouragement to Agriculture, and confequently to Population, we fhould confider it highly advantageous that a way be opened to allow them to export their Produce even to *Brazil*, in their own Veffels, under certain Duties, and fubject to the Supervifion both of the Director in *New Netherland*, and the Supreme

Council in *Brazil;* and to trade it off there, and to carry Slaves back in Return; which Privilege of failing with their own Ships from *New Netherland* to *Brazil,* fhould be exclufively allowed to Patroons and Colonifts, who promote the Population in *New Netherland,* and not to the Interlopers, who only carry Goods to and fro, without attending to Agriculture. By this Means not only would *Brazil* be fupplied with Provifions at a cheaper Rate, but *New Netherland* would by Slave Labor, be more extenfively cultivated than it has hitherto been, because the agricultural Laborers, who are conveyed thither at great Expense to the Colonists, sooner or later apply themselves to Trade, and neglect Agriculture altogether. Slaves, on the other Hand, being brought and maintained there at a cheap Rate, various other Descriptions of Produce would be raised, and by their Abundance be reduced in Price, so as to allow, when Occasion would offer, of their advantageous Exportation hither and to other Parts of Europe."

The Trade to *Africa* was opened, in 1652, to the Colonists, who

N. Y. Colonial MSS., IX, 53.

were permitted to import Slaves directly from that Country, within certain prescribed Limits. No immediate Action, however, followed this Permission; and it was not until the Year 1655 that Slaves began to be regularly imported into *New Netherland*.

It is to be borne in Mind, however, that during the War with *Spain*, Privateers swarmed among the *Caribbean Islands* and along the Spanish Main. These Vessels occasionally brought Prizes to *New Amsterdam*. After the Peace between the **United Netherlands** and

Introduction. xxiii

Spain, Hoſtilities were carried on between the latter Power and *France*. To the Privateers under the French Flag *New Amſterdam* was a neutral Port, where ſome of them occaſionally came and diſpoſed of their captured Negroes and other prize Goods.* *N. Y. Colonial Doc.*, I, 577, 578.

It has been aſſerted that Negroes were imported into *New Netherland* "often directly from *Guinea.*" This Allegation is baſed on the Deſpatch of 7th *April*, 1648, and on the *Bancroft's U. S.*, 1ſt Ed., II, 303.

---

* In 1642, the Privateer *La Garce* brought in a few Negroes, and in 1652 a Lot of *Forty-four* Negroes were brought in by another Privateer who had captured them from a Spaniard.

xxiv   *Introduction.*

mere Draft of a Contract in 1660 (*Infra*, P. 101, 169). But there is no Evidence that any Action followed the Permiſſion of 1648, and the Remonſtrance (*Infra*, P. 171), proves that the Contract not only had never been executed, but that the Parties declined executing it. The Records contain Inſtances of the Arrival of only two Veſſels at *New Amſterdam* "directly from *Guinea*" with Slaves. Theſe were the *Wittepaert* and *Gideon*. All other Importations of that Character were from *Curaçao*, except perhaps thoſe of the *Amandaré*, which moſt

Introduction. xxv

probably were brought from *Brazil.*

The Ventures and Veffels in this nefarious Commerce, belonged either to private Parties in *Holland,* or to the Weft India Company. "We have refolved," write the Directors at *Amfterdam* in 1661, "not only that Slaves fhall be kept in *New Netherland,* as we have heretofore ordered, but that they fhall moreover be exported to the Englifh and other Neighbours." The Spirit of Avarice and Greed deadened Confcience and fmothered all Feeling of Humanity; and "the Promotion of Agriculture, Trade, and Population" was the thin Covering which gloffed over the Infamy of the Trade.

In *November* 1661, the City of *New Amfterdam* became the Owner of three Negroes, which it obtained as a Prefent from the Director and Council. In 1664, "the City of *Amfterdam* did not blufh to own Shares in a Slave Ship, to advance Money for the Outfits, and to participate in the Returns." But to the Credit of *New Netherland,* it is to be recorded that no Ship nor Merchant belonging to that Colony,

Bancroft's U. S., 1ft Ed., II, 303.

had ever been engaged in the African Slave Trade. An Effort had, it is true, been made in *New Amsterdam* to embark in it, but the Project, fortunately for the Honor of the Country, fell through.

"Of a direct Voyage from *Guinea* to the Coast of the *United States* no Journal," says Mr. *Bancroft*, "is known to exist." The Papers now published will supply this Defect in some Degree; and the Journal of the Slaver *St. John*, though that Vessel was not destined for the Coast of *North America*, will give some Insight to the

History U. S.,
3d Edition, III, 405.

Horrors of the Middle Paſſage. *One hundred* and *ninety-five* human Beings were crammed into the Hold of that Veſſel. Bad Food, ſhort Allowance, Want of Water, foul Air, and Bloody Flux, were the Attendants on the Paſſage; and as a Conſequence, *fifty-ſix* per cent of the wretched Beings periſhed on the Voyage. Of the Balance, only one Negro eventually accrued to the Benefit of the Dutch; for, as a retributive Fate willed it, a Privateer, or Pirate, ſwooped down in the Vicinity of *Curaçao*, plundered every thing, and carried off the furviving Negroes "towards the Main."

No better Fortune awaited the Slaver, *The Arms of Amsterdam*. This Veffel brought *One hundred and one* Slaves from *Angola*, but on her Voyage to *Curaçao*, was overhauled by fome Englifh Privateers among the Weft India Iflands, captured and carried into *Virginia*.

Curaçao was, under the Dutch, what *Barbadoes* was fubfequently to the Englifh — the Slave Emporium to which Guineamen brought their Cargoes of human Flefh, to be thence diftributed throughout this Continent. And in the following Pages, the Reader will find ample Information regarding the active Trade in Slaves, which was carried on between that Ifland, *New Netherland*, and the Spanifh Poffeffions on the Main previous to 1665.

JOURNALS

OF THE

Voyages of the Slavers St. John
and Arms of Amsterdam.

JOURNAL

OF THE

SLAVER St. JOHN.

WE Weighed anchor, by order of the Honble Director, *Johan Valckenborch*, and the Honble Director *Jasper van Heuffen*, to proceed on our Voyage from *Elmina* to *Rio Reael*, to trade for Slaves for the Honble Company.

1659. Mar. 4.

A

1659. Mar. 8. Saturday. Arrived with our ship before *Arda*, to take on board the Surgeon's mate and a Supply of Tamarinds for the Slaves; sailed again next day on our Voyage to *Rio Reael*.

17. Arrived at *Rio Reael* in front of a village called *Bany* where we found the Company's Yacht, named the *Peace*, which was sent out to assist us to trade for Slaves.

April. Nothing was done except to trade for Slaves.

May 6. One of our seamen died; his name was *Claes van Diemen*, of *Durgerdam*.

22. Again weighed Anchor and

ran out of *Rio Reael* accompanied by the Yacht *Peace*; purchased there *two hundred and nineteen* head of Slaves, men, women, boys and girls, and proceeded on our course for the High land of *Ambosius*, for the purpose of procuring food there for the Slaves, as nothing was to be had at *Rio Reael*.

1659. May.

Monday. Arrived under the High land of *Ambosius* to look there for Victuals for the Slaves, and spent *seven* days there, but with difficulty obtained enough for the daily consumption of the Slaves, so that

26.

1659.
May. we resolved to run to *Rio Cammerones* to see if any food could be had there for the Slaves.

June 5. Thursday. Arrived at the *Rio Commerones* and the Yacht *Peace* went up to look for provisions for the Slaves. This day died our cooper, named *Peter Claeſſen*, of *Amſterdam*.

29. Sunday. Again resolved to proceed on our Voyage, as but little food was to be had for the Slaves in consequence of the great Rains which fell every day, and because many of the Slaves were suffering from the Bloody Flux in con-

sequence of the bad provisions we were supplied with at *El Mina*, amongst which were several barrels of Groats, wholly unfit for use. {1659. June.}

We then turned over to *Adriaen Blaes*, the Skipper, *One hundred* and *ninety* five Slaves, consisting of *Eighty one* Men, *One hundred* and *five* Women, *six* boys and *three* girls for which Bills of lading were signed and sent, one by the Yacht *Peace* to *El Mina* with an account of, and receipts for, remaining Merchandize.

Arrived at *Cabo de Loop de Gonsalvo* for wood and water. July 25.

1659.
July 27. Our Surgeon, named *Martin de Lanoy*, died of the Bloody Flux.

Aug. 10. Arrived the Company's Ship *Raven* from *Caſtle St. George d'el Mina*, homeward bound.

11. Again reſolved to purſue our Voyage towards the Iſland of *Annebo*, in order to purchaſe there Supplies for the Slaves. We have lain *Sixty* days at *Cabo de Loop* hauling wood and water. Among the Water barrels, forty were taken to pieces to be refitted, as our Cooper died at *Rio Cammerones*, and we had no other perſon capable of repairing them.

1659.
Aug. 15.
Arrived at the Island *An-nebo* where we purchased *One hundred* half tierces of little Beans, *twelve* Hogs, *five thousand* Cocoa nuts, *five thousand* Oranges, besides some other stores.

17.
Again hoisted Sail to prosecute our Voyage to the Island of *Curacao*.

Sept. 21.
The Skipper called the Ships officers aft, and resolved to run for the Island of *Tobago* and to procure Water there; otherwise we should have perished for want of water, as many of our Water casks had leaked dry.

1659.
Sept. 24. Friday. Arrived at the Ifland of *Tobago* and fhipped Water there, alfo purchafed fome Bread, as our hands had had no ration for three weeks.

27. Again fet fail on our Voyage to the Ifland of *Curacao*, as before.

Nov. 2. Loft our fhip on the Rifts of *Rocus*, and all hands immediately took to the Boat, as there was no profpect of faving the Slaves, for we muft abandon the Ship in confequence of the heavy Surf.

4. Arrived with the Boat at the Ifland of *Curacao*; the Hon[ble] Governor *Beck* ordered two

sloops to take the Slaves off the wreck, one of which sloops with *eighty four* slaves on board, was captured by a Privateer.

1659.
Nov.

LIST OF THE SLAVES

Who died on board the Ship St. John from 30th June to 29th October in the Year 1659.

1659.	Men.	Women.	Children.
June 30	3	2	
July 1	2	1	
3		1	
5		2	1
6		1	
7	1		
8	2	1	
9	2		
10		2	
12		1	
13	2		1
14	1		

1659.	Men.	Women.	Children.
July 16	3	2	
17	2		
18	3	1	
19	1	3	
20	1		
21	1	1	
23		2	
24	1	1	
25	2	1	
26	1		
28	3		
29		2	
Aug. 2	2		
3	1		
6	1		
8	2		1
9		1	
11		1	
16	1 man leaped overboard.		
18	1		
20		1	
22		1	
23		1	

1659.	Men.	Women.	Children.
Aug. 24	1		
29		1	
31	1	1	
Sept. 3		1	
6	2		
7	1		
8	1	1	
13	1	1	
14	2	2	1
16	1		
19	1		
23		2	
24	1	3	
26		1	
Oct. 1	2		
3	1	1	
4		1	
10	1	2	
12	1		
13	1		
19		1	
23	1		
29	1		
	59	47	4

On the *firſt* of November, two hours before day, have we loſt the Ship *St. John*, upon the Reef of *Rocus* and fled with the Boat to the Iſland of *Curaçao*, and left in the Ship *eighty five* Slaves, including Men, Women, Boys and Girls, and arrived on the *fourth* of this inſtant at *Curaçao*.

1659.
Nov. 1.

INFORMATION

Taken by Order of the Honble Director Matthias Beck *respecting the Capture of the Company's Negroes abandoned on board the Ship* St. John *on the Island of* Rocus, *and of the Company's Sloop which was sent to save them by the Honble Director* M. Beck *aforesaid.*

APPEARED *Jan van Gaelen* who was sent by the Hon. Director in the Company's Sloop, with the Skipper *Hans Marcussen Stuyve*, to aid in saving the aforementioned Slaves, and having sailed with the Skipper of the lost Ship and some of his Crew, from the Port here on the *Seventh* of November towards evening, came on the following Saturday in sight of *Bonaire*. When they were running towards the shore, they met an English Privateer or Rover whereof *Jan Pieterfen*, a native of Denmark, was Captain, who came off the land and had the weather-gage of them, and commanded them to strike, threatening to fire if they did not obey. And this Deponent coming on board the aforesaid Privateer, was asked, Whence came he and Whither was he bound? He answered, from *Curaçao* and was bound for *Bonaire*. Whereupon, the Captain of the Privateer asked, What business had he there? Thereupon, Deponent answered, To look up the Company's People. He, then, said, I am going with my Ship and remain you here on board and let the Vessel go on. Which they did and came to *Bonaire*. Being in the Roadstead with the aforesaid Vessel, on board of which were 5 or 6 of the Privateer's crew, one of the men of the wrecked Ship called out from the ſhore to thoſe of the Veſſel, as the Deponent hath afterwards underſtood, Did you bring along Skipper *Blaes*—to wit, the Skipper of the wrecked Ship— and have you been to *Rocus* to ſave the Negroes, who remained on board the Ship that lay ſtranded there? or, They ought firſt to go thither to ſave them. Whereupon the Privateers, who were in the bark, ſaid, addreſſing the Skipper of the wrecked Ship, Now, it is enough that we know that you are the Skipper of the wrecked Ship; and about two hours afterwards, the Privateer came with his Ship, named the *Caſtle frigate*, carrying *four* guns and about *thirty* men, into the Roadſtead where the Veſſel lay at anchor. Then his Fellows who were on board the Company's bark or Veſſel, called out; Captain, We have a good Prize — mentioning the Ship wrecked at *Rocus* — and having berated the Deponent for not having told him of what had occurred, was anſwered, He was not bound to do ſo; and at the same time requested and protested that he should let him go in order that he may prosecute the Voyage he had been sent on. Whereunto they were unwilling, but on the contrary, him detained by force, and on the following Sunday, dispatched the Vessel to *Little Curaçao* against his will where the aforesaid Privateer had his Lieutenant with a party of his men and a Pirogue to watch, as they said, the Company's vessels.

On the morning of the following Monday, the aforesaid Vessel returned with the

Lieutenant and Crew, leaving their Pirogue, which they had taken from the Spaniards, on the coaſt of *Curaçao*, ſtill at Anchor at *Little Curaçao*, and towards evening ſet ſail, taking with them by force the Company's Veſſel on board of which he put his crew, leaving in it only Skipper *Hans* aforeſaid with two men; and then took along by force on board his Ship the Deponent with the reſt of the Crew of the Veſſel and ſome belonging to the ſtranded Ship and proceeded on their Voyage to the Coaſt of *Caraccas* where coming, the Rover drove a Frigate afhore which was underftood to mount *fix* guns, and with the Company's veffel ftranded a Spanifh Pirogue, and afterwards proceeded to the little Ifland of *David*, where they came to an Anchor. Deponent having requefted with the other men to be fet on board their own Bark, they would confent that the Deponent only fhould go on board the bark or Veffel. The Rover remained there at Anchor and difpatched the Deponent with *fourteen* of faid Rover's crew in the Company's veffel to *Rocus*, with orders to feize the Slaves as a good Prize, even though the Bark named the *Young Brindle Cow*, whereof *Jan Ryckartfen* was Skipper, which had been fent thither by the Director to fave the aforefaid Slaves, might have them on board.

The abovementioned Bark had lain four days by the Wreck, and had made faft a line to it in order to get the Negroes on board by that means and fave them; but they could effect nothing through dread of the Negroes, and becaufe the hands on board the Bark were too few. They, therefore, refolved to await the arrival of the Veffel whereof the aforefaid *Hans Stuyve* was Skipper, in order thus to be ftronger in hands, and by that means better able to bring the Negroes on board. Then, on arriving there, the Rover's fourteen men did, in the prefence of this Deponent, run aboard them with the veffel, and attack and overpower them in a hoftile manner, and took the boats of the Bark and the Sloop, all the Property of the Company, and with them hauled the Negroes off the

Wreck to the number of *eighty four* and having loaded the Bark the *Brindled Cow* with them, proceeded to *David's iſland* where lay the Rover, who took all the Negroes on board.

Meanwhile, remained the Sloop or Veſſel with the Deponent at *Rocus*, pretending ſtill an inclination to ſave ſomething, and came the day following, to *David's iſland* having ſaved ſome cooking Kettles and Cordage which alſo they took away to the Rover. When this was accompliſhed, the Deponent enquired if they were satisfied and would permit him to depart with the aforesaid Veffel, or Company's Sloop. They answered, When they had hauled wood and water. Perfisting in his requeft, he at laft obtained for answer, That the Sloop was of ufe to them and they would not reftore it, and in cafe the Bark could be of fervice to them, they would retain her likewife, and further, every thing belonging to the Company on the way to or from *Curaçao*. However, fince fhe is of no ufe, you can go in her with all your folks and do'nt give much jaw, or you ſhall all march out naked, and do you go quietly on board and do not hoiſt a ſingle ſail until we are gone.

On the evening of the 23d. when he had ſailed, ſteering his courſe towards the Main-land, we took our departure and this day arrived here. And this he declares to have thus truly occurred, which if neceſſary he will confirm by oath; in preſence of *Theunis Lucaſſen* and *Peter de Leeuw*, as Witneſſes hereunto invited,

in *Fort Amſterdam* at *Curaçao*, the 25th *November* A° 1659.
 (Signed)
  JAN VAN GAELEN.
Witneſs
 Theunis Lucaſſen,
 Peter de Leeuw.
  In my preſence,
   NICOLAS HACK,
    Secretary.

Appeared *Jan Rykartſen*, Skipper of the Company's Sloop, *The Young Brindled Cow*, and ſays, that he by order of the Honble Director, had gone to *Aruba*. When there, received Instructions to proceed to *Rocus*, to save the Company's Slaves who were driven on shore there in the Ship *St. John*, coming from the Coast of *Guinea*. These orders I immediately executed. On arriving there, I used every diligence to reach the Wreck and so far succeeded as to get a line on board, and then two Negroes came swimming to the Boat by whom the line had been passed on board. It afterwards broke loose and in consequence of bad weather, I could not go on board. I, therefore, resolved to wait for the Company's veſſel whereof *Hans Marcuſſen Stuyve* was Skipper, who, I had been notified, would come to help to ſave the Slaves; the rather, becauſe my Crew being few in number ſtood, therefore, in fear of the Negroes.

On the 16th inſtant, arrived the Veſſel which attacked me in a hoſtile manner. Whereupon the Deponent demanded, What are you about? He ſaid, Shew your Sea brief which Deponent did. That, they ſaid, was well, and added, he might remain in their ſervice as long as he pleased, which he refused, being bound to serve not them, but the Honble Director in the Company's service upon which he was difpatched. Neverthelefs, he and his Crew were compelled to fubmit, and they forcibly took away his Boat, and with it the Company's Slaves and the Boat of the aforefaid Veffel, on board his own Ship, and commanded him to accompany them to *David's ifland*, where lay the Rover, called the *Caftle frigate*, the Captain whereof was *Jan Pieterfen* of *Colding*,* in *Denmark*, to whom the men belonged who maftered and captured the Company's Veffel aforefaid, and transferred the Slaves to the Ship. In the meanwhile, the aforefaid Veffel remained at *Rocus* with the Deponent's boat, in order, as they gave out, to fave by their means, more Property, and they, indeed, brought off two more Slaves, fome Elephants' teeth and other trifles, fo that altogether they took 84 Slaves and

* A City in the S. E. Corner of the Province of North Jutland, near the Little Belt.

2 sucking Children. They also took and carried off the aforesaid Company's Vessel whereof *Hans Marcussen Stuyve* was Skipper, and told me, the Deponent, that even had I had said Slaves on board the Bark on their arrival at *Rocus*, they should have taken them away by force, and declared them good prize, because I had no Commission, but only a Sea brief. And the Deponent says, that they offered him money for the service they had received from his Bark and Crew; this he refused to take, as such service was rendered

under compulfion, for he owed them no obedience and could not receive any thing for compulfory fervice. The Deponent alfo fays, that he hath given the Captain a note that he had received nothing from them, and likewife that the Captain of the aforefaid Rover had fent the Deponent on board, though the Crew of the aforefaid *Hans Marcuffen Stuyve's* Bark, belonging to the Company, had remained with him, and ordered me not to fail before he had departed, which was on the evening of the 23d of No-

vember, he fteering towards the Coaft, and we to this place where we arrived this date. And this he declares to be true and, if needs be, will confirm the fame by oath. *Curaçao* in *Fort Amfterdam* the 25th *November* A° 1659.
  (Signed)
      JAN RICKERTSEN.
Witnefs.
  Ghyfbert de Rofa
  Peter de Leeuw
    In prefence of me
      NICOLAS HACK,
        Secretary.

Appeared *Hans Marcuſſen Stuyve*, Skipper of the Company's Veſſel, and declared: On the 7th of November I ſailed hence by order of the Hon^(ble) Director for *Rocus*, there to ſave the Company's Slaves and other property from the Ship *St. John* coming there from *Guinea*. On the following day, arrived off *Bonaire* with the aforeſaid Bark, and met an Engliſh Privateer, or Rover, who having the wind of us obliged us to ſtrike. We then launched our Boat in which *Jan van Gaelen* went on board of him with two other hands, whom they detained, and ſent my Boat back with men to take poſſeſſion of my Bark which they did and carried us againſt our will to *Bonaire*, where being come, they put more hands on board and ſent this Deponent from there to *Little Curaçao* to fetch the Privateer's Lieutenant and ſome men thence, out of a Pirogue which they had taken from the Spaniards on the Coaſt of *Caraccas* and was ſtationed there to watch the Company's Veſſels going in and out.

Being come there, they came over in our Veffel and abandoned the Pirogue leaving her riding at anchor. Thus they returned to *Bonaire*, where the Rover rode at anchor, and being come there, they fet fail altogether, notwithftanding every Proteft againft the injuftice they did us, towards the Coaft of *Caraccas* where they drove a Spanifh Ship afhore, whilft we with our Sloop chafed a Pirogue afhore. Steering thence back we came to *Little David's ifland* where the Rover caft anchor, and having put more men on board of us, compelled us to go to *Rocus* to fave the Slaves from the wrecked Ship, and if they were already faved by the Company's Bark, whereof *Jan Ryckartfen* was Skipper, to capture and remove them by force. On arriving there, we found the Bark, which we immediately boarded and took by force, removing all the Slaves which had already been faved. But although they had been there *four* days before us, they were unable to effect any thing as the line they had fent on board the Wreck, had again broke loofe and they could not afterwards approach the Wreck in confequence of the violent wind. Only *two* Negro men came by fwimming on board of him; furthermore, finding themfelves too weak, they waited for our coming in order, being thus ftronger, to return and fave the Slaves &c, weather permitting. Boarding then the Bark, fhe was overpowered, as ftated, by force. Then taking their Shallop with ours, the Rover's crew, defpite our Protefts that we could not affift them, much lefs allow them to ufe our Vefsel, saved and brought on board the aforesaid Bark of Skipper *Jan Ryckertsen*, *Eighty two* Slaves and *two* Sucklings and steered away with them to *David's island*, where said Rover lay at anchor with his Vessel named the *Castle frigate*, the Captain whereof was *Jan Pietersen* of *Denmark*, and compelled us to remain with our Bark at *Rocus*, with the little Sloop of *Jan Ryckertsen* aforesaid, to save, as they said, some other Articles, which they did, namely, *eight* or *nine* little elephants' Teeth, *two* cooking Kettles, some tin Ware and

Cordage, and proceeded therewith to *David's ifland*, where the aforefaid Rover removed every thing from the faid Company's Veffels, and compelled us to remain until he had hauled Wood and Water. Nay, he would pay the Deponent for his trouble and the ufe of the Veffels and Sloop, which he would not accept, giving for anfwer, That they were fent out not on this, but the Company's fervice by the Honble Director *Matthias Beck*, and that force and violence had been employed againft them. Whereupon the

Captain of the Rover was greatly irritated, and carried off the Deponent's Veffel, notwithftanding he had more than three times exhibited to him his Commiffion which the Honble Director had given him, acknowledging even that the Commiffion was valid and that he was a Free man, and had nothing to fay againft him. All which notwithftanding, he afterwards carried off my Veffel with him, faying, He had need of it, and made me vacate it with my Men, permitting us only to take our Clothing, and then put us on board *Jan Ryckertfen's* Bark. The Deponent further faith, that he was compelled per force to fign a Note, not knowing its contents, for it was written in Englifh, and this Deponent does not underftand the Englifh language. And having been ordered not to fail before the Rover left, which was on the evening of the 23d *November* inftant, fteering his courfe towards the Main, we, with the aforefaid Bark of *Jan Ryckertfen* leaving behind one of our Sailors named *Jacob Pieterfen* of *Belcom*, who voluntarily remained with them, fteered towards this Harbor, where we arrived in safety this day. And this he declares to be true and will confirm the same if needs be, by oath; in presence of *Ghysbert de Rosa* and *Peter de Leeuw* as witnesses hereunto invited. *Curaçao* in *Fort Amsterdam* the 25th *November* A° 1659.

 (Signed)

  This is the mark ᛭ of Skipper
 Hans Marcussen Stuyve
Witness Ghysbert de Rosa
   Peter de Leeuw
In presence of me
  Nicolaes Haek, *Secretary.*

Appeared *Adriaen Blaes van der Veer*, and faith, that he was commanded by *Johan Valckenburch* General of *El Mina* and the *Gold Coaſt*, on the 4th of *March* laſt to fail as Skipper of the Ship *St. John*, from the Roadſtead of the *Caſtle del Mina* aforefaid, with Commiſſary *Johan Froon* and the accompanying Sailors, in the Company's fervice, to the *Calabari* or *Rio Real*, there to trade for Slaves and to proceed with them, by order of the aforefaid General, to this place. In obedience to thefe orders, *Two hundred* and *nineteen* Slaves big and little, were actually traded and purchased, wherewith we sailed in order to proiecute our Voyage and carry out our Instructions. Not obtaining at the *Calabari* such sufficiency of provisions as this Voyage demanded, for the sustenance of the aforesaid Slaves, we resolved to go to the Highland of *Ambosius* where we were unable to procure any Provisions, as was our desire. We, therefore went to the River *Camerones*, where we obtained a few Articles, but not as much as we wanted.

Neverthelefs, we purfued our Voyage towards *Capo de Lopo Gonfalves*, at which place we took in Wood and Water, and thence ftood acrofs although experiencing great mifery and want of food, to *Anabo*, where we got fome Provifions and went on our Voyage and made land in the month of *October* laft at the Ifland of *Tobago*, the greater portion of the Slaves having died from Want and Sicknefs, in confequence of fuch a very long Voyage, fo that we faved only *Ninety* Slaves, out of the whole Cargo. Having taken in wood and water and a few Refreshments from the surrounding Islands, we set sail and after we fixed our course on the *first* instant, west by south, we ran ashore, two hours before day, on one of the Rifts of *Rocus*, on the North East side of the Island. Perceiving our danger, we saved ourselves with all the Crew in the Boat, leaving the Negroes in the Ship, taking our course to this place, in order to inform the Hon[ble] Director *M. Beck* of our Misfortune. After we had left some of the men at *Bonayre*, because the Boat was too heavily laden with the Crew, we arrived here on the *fourth* inſtant. Having reported ourſelves to the aforeſaid Honble Director, he diſpatched me with the above Boat to *Aruba*, whither the Company's Veſſels had ſailed, the day before, on the Company's buſineſs, with orders to proceed in ſaid Veſſels with five of my men, and *Jan van Gaelen*, the Company's ſervant. Arriving there on the following day, we went over in the Company's Veſſel, whereof *Hans Marcuſſen Stuyve* was Skipper, with *Jan van Gaelen*, and two of my

G

Crew, and the other three of my men in the Bark, called *The Young Brindled Cow*, of which *Jan Ryckertsen* was Skipper, all in the service of the Company.

We pursued our Voyage without any mishap, pursuant to the orders we had received from the aforesaid Honble Director here, and so on to *Rocus*, to save the Slaves and Ship's property, and having sailed on the evening of the *seventh* after remaining half an hour here, we arrived in the afternoon of the following day off *Bonayre* where we met an

English Privateer, who having the wind of us, overtook us and compelling us to ſtrike and to ſend off a Boat, the aforeſaid *Jan van Gaelen* went on board him, who told him, we came from *Curaçao* and were going to *Bonayre*. Thereupon, the ſaid Privateer diſpatched in our Boat, in which *Jan van Gaelen* whom he detained, had gone to his Ship, on board our Veſſel a party of his men to ſearch for Pieces of Eight which, they ſaid, we had. Then not finding any, as we had none, they forced us to run with them up the Roadstead of *Bonayre*, where we arrived about *two* hours before the Privateer. Some of my Men who were on shore, not knowing any thing of these proceedings, called out, If I were on board? The Privateer's men taking up the word before me, asked, Who? Thereupon they answered, The Skipper of the Ship wrecked at *Rocus*, adding, Had we been to the Slaves, or were we going to save them? The Privateers answered, That they were going to save them; manifesting great joy thereat, saying, when the Privateer caft anchor, Captain, we have a good Prize. Thereupon they forced the Deponent to go on board the Rover which was a fmall Frigate, carrying *four* guns, and about *thirty* men, whereof *Jan Pieterfen*, a native of *Denmark*, was Captain. This Veffel was called *The Caftle frigate*. Coming on board, the Captain enquired, How many Negroes he had left on his Ship? Deponent anfwered, *Eighty*. When he heard that, he fent the Veffel in which the Deponent came, to *Little Curaçao*, to bring his Lieutenant and fome of his men, who were lying there in a Periauger, which they had taken from the Spaniards, to watch the Company's Veſſels. Meanwhile this Deponent remained on board the Rover, and they returning to us in the Roadſtead of *Bonayre*, the Rover permitted this Deponent to go back to the Bark, on board of which ſtill were, Skipper *Hans Marcuſſen* aforeſaid, with one of his hands, who had been compelled to go to *Little Curaçao* to fetch his Lieutenant and men. To this Veſſel I came, as ſtated, from the aforeſaid Rover with two of my Crew, being then in all *five* fervants of the Company on faid Company's Veffel. The Captain of the Rover having then placed his Lieutenant and Pilot, with fome of his hands, on board the Bark, we fet fail under compulfion, leaving *Jan van Gaelen* and fome of our men behind, whom the Rover retained by force on board his Ship, not heeding any protefts or requefts as free men, which they themfelves admitted us to be, having cognizance of the Commiffion granted by the Hon[ble] Director to the aforesaid *Hans Marcuſſen Stuyve*, as Skipper of the aforesaid Veſſel, and that therefore, they used force and violence towards us who were not in any manner in their service, but indeed in that of the Company, to whom alone we owed Obedience, and that for the purpose of executing the orders of the Honble Director, to which end and to no other, were we sent out. All this notwithstanding, were we compelled to accompany the aforesaid Rover who set sail at the same time, taking his course towards the Main land of *Ca-*

raccas where he drove on fhore a Spanifh Ship mounting *fix* guns, and with our Bark, in our prefence and before Deponent's face, drove a Spanifh Periauger afhore. Thence they and the Rover forced us to crofs over and caft anchor under *Little David's ifland*, and having put more people in our Bark, until fhe numbered in all fourteen men, whilft he remained there at Anchor, we fet fail for *Rocus*.

On arriving at that place, we found the other of the Company's Veffels, named *The Young Brindled Cow*, whereof

Jan Ryckertſen aforeſaid was Skipper, with three of my men on board, who accompanied him to *Aruba*, out of my Boat. They went thither, as already ſtated, by command of the aforeſaid Hon[ble] Director, alſo with orders to no other intent than to ſave the aforeſaid Slaves &c, and had lain there four Days and had ſo far ſucceeded as to paſs a line on board my Ship, two of the Negroes coming on board ſwimming. The aforeſaid line breaking looſe, and finding themſelves too weak in conſequence of the ſtrong wind, the Men refolved to wait our arrival, having been informed of our approach, fo as, when thus reinforced and the Weather would moderate, to fave with our Sloop and Boat the aforefaid furviving Slaves &c. from my Ship which alfo belonged to the Company. Then they, the Rover's men, who were on board our Bark, fuppofing that the aforefaid Skipper *Jan Ryckertfen* with his Crew and my three men had faved all, coming to them went on board with our Bark, according to the orders they had to that effect, from their

Captain, who had been informed of the departure of the aforesaid Company's Bark and the purport for which we were sent out, by a Frieslander named *Jacob Petersen* from *Belcom*, a Sailor in the Company's service, under Skipper *Hans Marcussen Stuyve*, who had voluntarily deserted to them on the same day that we came on board the Rover. Which orders were to board them, to see if they had saved the Slaves &c. and to seize and remove them. They accordingly did attack them in a hostile manner in the prefence of the Deponent and four other of the Company's Servants who could not refrain from remonftrating againft the injuftice which they demonftrated they were doing. Finding that no more than the two aforefaid Slaves had been faved, they took away, per force our Boat together with *Jan Ryckertfen's* Boat, all the property of the Company appertaining to the aforefaid Veffels, and with them, the weather moderating fomewhat, removed the Slaves from my Ship, making ufe for that purpofe of one of my Matroffes named

Martin Michielsen van Hulst, who was on board *Jan Ryckertsen*'s Bark aforesaid. By his assistance, for the Negroes knew him and called him by name, the aforesaid *Jan Ryckertsen* got the line on board, and in like manner accompanied one of the Rovers at the time all the Slaves &c. were on board, and then came again swimming on board the Lieutenant of the Rover with *two* of his men, who then numbered *four*, having again brought a rope on board from the Company's Vessel by which they let all the Negroes who were capable of swimming, swim off to the Rift, whilst they brought those who could not swim in a Boat belonging to the aforesaid Vessels, to the same Rift, and having meanwhile made the other Boat dry inside the Rift, they brought in her on board the aforesaid *Jan Ryckertsen's* Bark, *eighty two* Slaves and *two* Sucklings. And this Deponent having, before they removed any of the Slaves, requested of the Lieutenant and his men belonging to the Rover, permission to go with his aforesaid Matross, he was unwilling to grant it until some of the Slaves had been removed out of the Ship, so that when this Deponent went on board his Ship there remained on board no more than about *thirty* Slaves. After all the Negroes had been removed from his Ship, this Deponent was conveyed to *Jan Ryckertsen's* Bark, with the Instructions which General *Johan Valckenburgh* had given him, together with all the Papers and Accounts of the said Commissary, relating to his freight and other business matters, done pursuant to the Company's orders. Then the Depopent was conveyed by them with the aforefaid Bark and Negroes, to *David's ifland*, where the Rover lay at anchor waiting for us, leaving behind them the Veffel whereof *Jan Marcuffen Stuyve* is Skipper, to fave *two* Negroes whom the Deponent had left on board when he quit the Ship. That Veffel joined them the next day at *David's ifland*, bringing along the *two* aforefaid Slaves, fome Kettles, Rope and about 70 pounds of Elephants' teeth, alfo fome Flags, Compaffes and other articles. The Rover having removed the Slaves and every thing elfe out of the Company's Veffels, took from the Deponent the Inftructions given him by the General, with all the Commiffary's Papers, notwithftanding the protefts and requefts to the contrary, giving the Deponent for anfwer, that all belonged to him. He, moreover, commanded them to remain by him until he had hauled Wood and Water, and afterwards took *Hans Marcuffen Stuyve's* Veffel, faying he required her. He then made the Deponent remain on board *Jan Ryckert-*

sen's Bark, compelling him to make room for said *Hans Marcussen Stuyve* with all his Crew and some of the Deponent's men. Then he ordered them not to sail for this Place until he had taken his departure, which was on the 23d instant, steering his course towards the Main. And this Deponent with his Crew and that of the Company's Bark, took their course with the aforesaid *Jan Ryckertsen's* Bark, to this Place where they arrived in safety on the 25th instant.

This he declares to be the truth, and to have thus oc-

curred, and will if needs be, confirm the fame on oath, in prefence of Mr *Gyfbert de Rofa* and *Peter de Leeuw*, witneffes hereunto invited. *Curaçao* in *Fort Amfterdam* the 27th *November* A° 1659.
  (Signed)
        Adriaen Blaes.
Witneffes.
  Ghyfbert de Rofa
  Peter de Leeuw
    In my prefence
      Nicolaes Haek,
          Secretary.

PROCLAMATION.

MATTHIAS BECK, *in the service of their High Mightinesses the Lords States General of the free* United Netherlands *and of the Honble General Incorporated West India Company, Governor over the* Curaçao *Islands*, GREETING:

BE *it known*, that one *Jan Pieterſen* of *Coling* in *Denmark*, styling himself Commander of a Ship called *The Castle Frigate*, having with him some Englishmen, Frenchmen and Dutchmen, who are cruising with him on this Coast in the Ship aforesaid, hath dared to attack the Company's Vessels near *Bonayre* and *Rocus*, and forcibly to take possession thereof, and with them and the Company's Men to take by force, among others, *eighty four* healthy Negroes out of the Company's Ship, called *The St. John*, coming from the Coast of *Guinea*, which was wrecked on the Rifts of *Rocus*, where one of the aforesaid Company's Ships was already engaged in saving said Negroes for the Company, whofe Property they were, with all that was in the Ship, to bring them here to *Curaçao*, for which purpofe they were exprefsly fent hence thither; Regardlefs whereof, the aforefaid *Jan Pieterfen* hath not only prevented the Company's Veffels executing their Inftructions and Orders, but hath made himfelf Mafter of faid Veffels, and with them and Boats, ftole not only the faid Negroes and every thing elfe, but in addition thereto carried off one of the Company's beft failing Veffels called *The Young Oftrich*, to the great damage of the Honble Company, and appropriated the fame to himfelf as good booty, fo as all is to be feen by the Informations, Relations, Reports and Delarations of the Skipper and Crews of the Veffels aforefaid.

And *Whereas* the aforefaid *Jan Pieterfen* and his Men have heretofore committed fimilar acts under irregular Commiffion and perfift in the fame courfe, efpecially as public Pirates, by the feizure of the Company's Veffel and Negroes, and have threatened to continue fo to do; And *Whereas* among others, one of the Company's Matroffes named *Jan Pieterfen* of *Belcom*, a Frieflander, being in our actual fervice, having failed as Matrofs on board the Company's ftyger fchuit, *The Young Brindled Cow*, hath voluntarily gone over to this Pirate, difregarding the Allegiance, Plight and Oath, whereby he was bound to the Company, but on the contrary, as appears by Information, hath acted and is ftill acting, as a Spy for thefe Pirates; All which and what precedes are matters of very ill confequence, of ferious damage and moment to the Honble General Incorporated Weſt India Company, who will not fail to expreſs their higheſt Indignation on this ſubject, and endeavor by all ways and means, not only to make good and to procure an indemnity for their damages and loſſes already ſuffered by the ſtealing of their Veſſel and Negroes, ſo illegally purloined from them, but above all, to procure that ſuch Rovers ſhall be puniſhed as Pirates and Robbers, according to their deſerts, as an Example to others.

To this end, therefore, with the advice of Our Council, upon the certain Proofs and Reports to Us rendered, We, being unwilling to lofe any time in overhauling the faid Sea Robbers, have Refolved and concluded, in the Name and on the Behalf of the Lords Principals, their High Mightineffes the Lords States General, and the Honble General Incorporated Weft India Company, for their protection and the Public Good, hereby to warn all the Company's Captains, and Ships as well as Private Skippers and Ships and Veffels at prefent lying or about to come, within this Harbor, who owe allegiance to their High Mightineffes the Lords States General and are in the fervice of the Honble General Incorporated Weft India Company not only to be on their guard againft the aforefaid Pirates and Sea Robbers, but fhould they meet them at Sea, them to attack, openly and with force and arms, and bring them in here to *Curaçao*, or if they fall in with them at any of the *Leeward Iflands*, to complain of them to the Governors and

Magiſtrates at ſuch place where they happen to find them, according to the Proofs thereof in exiſtence, and to procure that ſuch Juſtice may be inflicted upon them as the Informations ſhall juſtify. Requeſting all Generals, Governors and Commanders both on Sea and on Land, to whom theſe Our Letters for the execution of the premiſes ſhall be ſhown, to adminiſter good Law and Juſtice to them. Such will We reciprocate on like Occaſion. Thus done and enacted on the Iſland *Curaçao* in *Fort Amſterdam* the 5th *December*, Aº 1659.

Vice Director BECK *to the* WEST INDIA COMPANY, *Chamber at Amsterdam.*

Curaçao, 5 January, 1660.

Honorable, Respected, Wise, Prudent and most Discreet Sirs,

Gentlemen,

BY the Ships *King Solomon* and *St. John* 3d September, was my last to your Honors, to which I refer.

* * * * * * * * *

I despatch these few lines at present by the bearers hereof, the Commissary and

Skipper of the Ship *St. John*, who coming from the Coaſt of *Guinea* with Negroes were wrecked on *Rocus* on the Voyage hither, leaving behind them ſome *Eighty* living Slaves, beſides many and a greater number of dead ones who were ſtarved on the way for want of food. Your Honors will pleaſe ſee in the accompanying Papers what diligence I have uſed to ſave thoſe living; alſo, how the Sea Rovers, of whom I heretofore adviſed you, have carried off not only the Negroes, but alſo the beſt of the Company's Barks, as appears by the said Papers, to which and to the verbal Report of the aforesaid Commissary and Skipper I, for brevity sake, refer.

With submission to your Honors, it would in my opinion not be unadvisable if a suitable well fitted Vessel or Yacht could be obtained, carrying half a dozen guns. She could be employed in bringing Horses from *Aruba* to *Bonayre* and this place, many of which are now bitten to death by the Rattlesnakes there, and on such occurring occasions be manned with hands sufficient to overhaul such Sea Rovers, and used for various other purposes.

As it is in the highest degree necessary to look after the Sea Rovers, in order at least to imprefs them with the fear of approaching so near us, I have chartered a small private Boat, mounting *six* guns, strongly manned and double armed to look up the aforesaid Sea Robbers at the place where, we presume, they are sojourning, in the hope of obtaining not only some advantage over them, but if we should catch the Ringleaders, of having such punishment inflicted on them as would serve as an example to others. Herein we shall not fail in our duty.

Director BECK *to Director*
STUYVESANT.
Curaçao, 4. February, 1660.
Sir,

MY laſt dated 23 Auguſt and 10th September were ſent your Honor by the Ship *Sphera Mundi* as per copies annexed, to which I refer. Since then, I have had none of yours to acknowledge. Therefore this ſhall be the ſhorter, the rather as I tranſmit encloſed to you open the accompanying deſpatch to our Lords Maſters, in order that you may, yourself, be able to see from it what transpired here, and having taken cognizance thereof to seal and send it by the first sailing Ship to Amsterdam to the Lords Masters.

As your Honor will be able to glean from the Informations and Papers inclosed therein, what sort of Sea Rovers here have taken the Company's Negroes and Bark, among which visitors was also to be found one *Pickled Herring*, who formerly went privateering with Captain *Beaulieuw*, and now and then makes his appearance in your Honor's jurifdiction in *New Netherland*, and poffibly fome of the Ringleaders of them may land there, we wifh, in fuch cafe, that they were made known to you, to the end that you may caufe fuch Juftice to be adminiftered to them as they deferve.

If your Honor have an opportunity of writing to *Jamaica*, where I partly underftand thefe Rovers have arrived, and where they have no Counter party and can make fuch Reprefentation as they pleafe to the General there, your Vigilance might effect a great deal of good by tranfmitting a Letter on the fubject to him, which fhall alfo be done here when an opportunity offers.

* * * * * * * * *

I greatly defired that the Ships expected with Negroes had arrived, in order to enable me to fend your Honor fome lufty fellows, but none have come up to this date, although looked for every day. We muft poftpone doing fo until the next opportunity, God willing.

JOURNAL

OF THE SLAVER

The Arms of Amsterdam

AND

HER CAPTURE.

JOURNAL

OF THE SLAVER

The Arms of Amsterdam,

AND

HER CAPTURE.

PAULUS *Heyn Ridder* from *Staden*, aged about 51 years, Pilot of the Ship the *Arms of Amsterdam*, and *Leendert Jacques van Cuelen*, born at *Amsterdam*, aged about 26 years, Assistant Commissary, who arrived here yesterday from *Virginia*, in Mr. *Foscom*'s Bark,

M

appeared at the Meeting of the Director General and Council of *New Netherland*, and made known and declared as followeth:

That they, the Deponents, set sail from the *Castle del Mina* on the 21st *February* last in the service and for the account of the Honble Incorporated West India Company, Chamber at Amsterdam, in the Ship the *Arms of Amsterdam*, at which time *Jan Gerritsen Nuchteren*, who died on the passage on the   , was Skipper, with orders and command from the Honble General *Jan Valckenburgh* to repair to *Loango* in *Angola*, to take in a cargo of Slaves there, and convey them to the Ifland of *Curaçao*.

April 15. Having arrived at *Loango* and taken on board 101 head of Slaves there for account of the abovementioned Company,

On the 28th of faid month, again fet fail for *Curaçao*.

June 20. Sighted *Curaçao*, but could not reach faid Ifland in confequence of the ftrong Current and ftiff Eaft wind. Having vainly endeavored, during three days and three nights, to laveer, and Water beginning to get very low, we were necessitated to change our course, and thus

July 2, came to the Salt ground of *Cayman*, which is one of the Cayman Islands, where, whilst engaged in taking Water and some Turtle on board, on

July 6, about noon, *five* Ships came to anchor there; *four* with English flags and one under Portuguese colors, which last, called the *Maria* of *London*, whereof one *Robert Douwneman* was Captain, after she had taken some hands on board from the other Ships, immediately weighed anchor again, and came down on the Deponent's Ship, calling out, "Strike for the King of Portugal;" and at once, without giving time to ſtrike, fired a ſhotted Cannon and a diſcharge of Muſketry killing two Negroes dead, and wounding one Dutchman. After having thus fired, came ſtraight on board, ſeized the Ship and Negroes, forced the Crew to go to the Ship aforeſaid and plundered every thing. The Captains of the four Engliſh Ships abovementioned, one of whom was called Captain *Gey* and another, Captain *Brommert*, got some of the Negroes because they had furnished him men, but the Deponents do not know how many. After they had lain there some days, said Captain having first dismantled his own Frigate set her on fire, and

July 18, sailed thence with the aforesaid Ship, *The Arms of Amsterdam*, having enlisted some of the Sailors, giving out that he intended to sail to *Montserrat* in the Caribbean Islands, but as the Ship was a poor Sailer, and Water was short, he set sail for *Virginia* and arrived

September 10, in the Bay there.

September 19, arrived at *Elizabeth's river*, whence the Deponent went to *Nancimon*.

October 6, departed thence for this place in Mr. *Fofcom's* Bark, and arrived here yesterday.

All which they declared to be true and truthful. In testimony whereof thefe prefents are figned by them in *Fort Amfterdam* in *New Netherland*, the 13th *October* A° 1663.

FINIS.

APPENDIX.

N

ADDITIONAL PAPERS

RELATIVE TO

The Slave Trade

UNDER THE DUTCH.

Directors at Amsterdam to Director STUYVESANT.

* * * * *

[1646.] HAVING obferved that more Negroes could be profitably traded off there than were carried thither in the Ship *Tamandare*, we fhall pay attention that for the future more Negroes fhall be conveyed thither.

Bill of Sale of a Negro.

BEFORE me *Cornelis Van Tienhoven*, Secretary of *New Netherland*, appeared *Fredrick Lubberſen*, who declared to have ſold unto *Richard Lord*, a Negro named *Anthony*, which Negro, he the Grantor hereby conveys and tranſports in right ownerſhip to the abovenamed *Richard Lord*, who ſhall be at liberty to uſe the ſaid Negro during his life, at all ſuch work, as he, *Richard Lord*, ſhall think proper. He *Fredrick Lubberſen* declares from this day forward to deſiſt from all property in the ſaid Negro. In teſtimony whereof theſe preſents are ſigned by *Fredrick Lubberſen* and witneſs hereunto invited, 28th 9ber 1646.

   FRERICK LUBBERTSEN.
To my knowledge,
  CORNELIS VAN TIENHOVEN, *Secretary*.
  ADRIAEN VAN TIENHOVEN, *Witneſs*.

Directors at Amsterdam to Director STUYVESANT.

EFFORTS are juft now making at the *Hague* before their High Mightineffes to effect a general Reform in all the Colonial poffeffions of this Company, and *New Netherland* alfo was remembered on that occafion. It has been already provifionally refolved that all Colonifts of that Country fhall be empowered to export their products of Flour, Fifh, Beef, Pork, Peas, Beans, &c., in their own, or in chartered Ships to *Brafil*, and *Angola*; that faid Ships may again take freight from *Brafil* to this Country, but that thofe who have completed their trade in *Angola* fhall be at liberty to convey Negroes back home to be employed in the cultivation of their lands. By this refolution Your Honor will obferve that we ourfelves are at liberty to fend a Ship with all forts of Provifions to *Angola* and to convey Negroes back in return. Therefore pleafe to embrace this opportunity as quickly as poffible with the Provifions which you fay you will have remaining.

Amfterdam, 7th *April,* 1648.

Directors at Amfterdam to the Commonalty at the Manhattans.

* * * * *

AND in order that you may be the more fully affured of our good intention, we do hereby confent that the Commonalty yonder fhall have liberty to repair to the

Coast of *Angola* and *Africa*, and transport thence as many Negroes as they will make use of for the cultivation of their Lands, on the Conditions and regulations which are sent herewith to the Director.

* * * * *

Amsterdam, 4th April, 1652.

Directors at Amsterdam to Director STUYVESANT.

* * * * *

WE have by contract given and granted to some private Merchants permission empowering them to repair to the Coast of *Africa* to trade for Slaves there, and to carry and convey them to the *West Indies* and the Islands situate thereabout, and as we expect that the aforesaid

Ships or fome of them will go to *New Netherland* to fell their Slaves alfo to the Inhabitants there, in fuch cafe we defire and requeft that Your Honor will not demand any Duties from them, but lend them all reafonable Affiftance, in order to the removal of every obftacle which might prove a hinderance to Agriculture. This for your information and notification.*

* * * * *

Amfterdam, this 6th June, 1653.

* NOTE BY DR. VANDERKEMP.—Here are reported unqueftionable Facts that the *Dutch* were the chief Supporters of the Slave Trade, ftamping their Seal on the Declaration of one of the Magiftrates of *Amfterdam* to Prince *Frederick*, "that he would fend a Cargo to *Hell* at the Rifk of fingeing his Sails if he were fure of a profperous Voyage."

Refolution of the Affembly of the XIX.

Monday, 15 September, 1653.

THE Committee appointed for this purpofe reports with regard to the Ninth Article relative to Privateering, as the refult of their deliberations, that the Regulation of the year 1646 on this fubject ought to remain in force, but in order to encourage Individuals, in this critical conjuncture, to equip Veffels to annoy the Enemy, it might be permitted, befides lowering the duties granted in 1652, that the following alterations be provifionally adopted :

※ ※ ※ ※ ※

5.

The Negroes coming in prizes from beyond the Seas, and nothing elſe, may be exported, with the conſent of the Government in *Brazil*, to all ſuch places as the intereſted may deem proper.

6.

The duties which the Company receives from all prize goods brought in and mentioned in the aforeſaid rule, Negroes included, ſhall be reduced to *ten* per cent, and no more.

Directors at Amſterdam to Director STUYVESANT.

* * * * *

26. AFTER cloſing and diſpatching the duplicate hereof which goes by the Ship *The Black Eagle*, we have on the Petition of ſome private Merchants, viz., *Jan*

Sweerts and *Dirck Pieterfen Wittepaert*, and in order to promote Population and Agriculture there, confented and allowed that they may go with their Ship the *Wittepaert* to the Coaft of *Africa*, and having trafficked for Slaves there, convey the fame to *New Netherland* to be fold to the Inhabitants there, provided that of the Goods and returns proceeding from faid Slaves, and which fhall be brought back in the abovementioned Ship, there fhall be paid to the Company the lawful Duties fixed thereon, or otherwife the ordinary Tonnage duty according to the regulation enacted at the Coaft of *Africa*, at the Company's option, as appears by the annexed extract of Refolutions adopted on the 19th of this month.

* * * * *

Amfterdam, 23d *November*, 1654.

Resolution of the Amsterdam Chamber of the West India Company.

No. 26.

Thursday, the 19th November, 1654.

MR. *Jan de Sweerts* and *Dirck Pieterfen Wittepaert* appeared before the Assembly, and requested permission to proceed hence with their Ship the *Witte paert*, to the Coast of *Africa* for Slaves, and to dispose of these in *New Netherland*, on payment of the ordinary Tonnage, or the Duty fixed therefor. Question being put, considerable discussion ensued, and as it was understood that such would tend to the increase of Population and advancement of said Place, the fame was confented to, on condition that the Company fhall have the option, on the arrival of faid Ship, which muft come in here, to collect the proper Duties of the Goods which fhe is to bring with her, or the ordinary Tonnage duty, according to the Regulation enacted on the Coaft of *Africa*, with which the abovementioned Meff[rs] *Jan de Sweerts* and *Dirck Pieterfen Wittepaert* are fatisfied.

Ordinance impofing a Duty on Exported Slaves.

Friday, 6. *Auguft,* 1655.

WHEREAS the Director General and Council of *New Netherland* find that the Negroes lately arrived here from the Bight of *Guinea* in the Ship *Witte Paert*, have been tranfported and carried hence without the Honble Company or the Inhabitants of this Province having derived any Revenue or benefit therefrom, the Director General and Council have refolved and concluded that there fhall be paid at the General Treafury 10 per cent of the value or purchafe money of the Negroes who fhall be carried away or exported from here elfewhere beyond the Jurifdiction of *New Netherland*. Dated as above.

    P. STUYVESANT,
    NICASIUS DE SILLE,
    LA MONTAGNE.

Resolution of the Director General and Council of New Netherland.

Tuesday, 24th August, 1655.

THE Petition of *Edmund Scharburgh* being read, requesting permission to depart from this place to Virginia with his Vessel and some Negroes he has purchased, this Apostile was given:

The Request is granted, on condition that the Petitioner give bail in the sum of five thousand Pounds sterling, not to enter the South Bay or River, and that his Crew promise under Oath not go there, nor communicate any intelligence by Sea or Land to any person whomsoever.*

---

* Referring to the Expedition against the Swedes, on the Delaware River, then about to sail.

Resolution of the Chamber at Amsterdam.

Monday, 3d. April, 1656.

IT being represented that a Ship, with the consent of the Directors of *Medenblick*, depending on the Chamber of *West Friesland* and *The North Quarter*, has sailed to the Coast of *Africa* for Slaves, with intention to sell them at the Island of *Curaçao*,* or to trade them on the Main, it is resolved to oppose the aforesaid sale or barter, and to write to Vice Director *Beck* there, to detain the aforesaid Ship and Slaves and to proceed therewith so and in

---

* *Curaçao* was exclusively under the Direction of the Chamber at *Amsterdam*, and it may be inferred from the above that the exclusive Control of the Dutch Slave Trade was also vested in that Chamber.

fuch manner as he fhall find confiftent with law.

Vice Director BECK *to the Directors at Amfterdam.*

Curaçao, 11. *June*, 1657.

Honorable, Refpected, Wife, Prudent and moft Difcreet Gentlemen.

Gentlemen,

MY laft to your Honors was by way of the *Caribbean Iflands*, which I hope has been received long ere this. Since then fafely arrived here the Freight-boat with thofe who were commiffioned and fent for purpofes explained in our previous difpatch, from this place, to the *Caraquas*, the principal Capital of the Main, lying neareft this

P

Ifland, bringing with them the written Anfwer of the Governor of faid locality, who, as reprefented, was favorably inclined to what was propofed to him in our letter, yet dared not manifeft fuch in public, becaufe, as he alleges, of the Limits agreed upon and concluded in the Articles or Treaty of Peace between his Royal Majefty of *Spain* and their High Mightineffes the Lords States General. The original Letter received from there, mentioned above, goes herewith, together with the Relation and Verbal Report of the difpofition in which our two Commiffioners, who were fent thither, found them. Neverthelefs, in order to avoid fufpicion and ar-reft, and on account of fome Ships lying there, they did not find it expedient to deliver the principal and feparate Memorial entrufted to them to the Governor and Chief Authorities of that place, the rather as no occafion or opportunity prefented itfelf; for they had not been further than the beach in the Harbor and under the Fortrefs, whence they had been again difpatched without having been invited to *Caraquas*, the Capital. They were, however, by order and command of the Governor of *Caraquas* courteoufly entertained by the chief officers of the Fortrefs and place, of the Village and Harbor where they lay and were offered every thing they ftood in need of for the profecution of their Voyage to *Euftatius*. They report that they have had many inquiries and folicitations for goods, fuch as Silks, Linens and Hats, but they excufed themfelves; trade to their Coafts, Harbors and Territories not being permitted, they dared not bring any thing with them. But on the other hand, if they had an opportunity, and would pleafe to come to *Curaçao*, to purchafe Negroes and Merchandize, they would be welcome there and accommodated to their fatisfaction either for Specie, Hides, Tobacco or other commodities faleable in Europe. They had communicated to divers individuals the feparate Memorial with which they had been entrufted, and had, according to opportunity, divulged it to them as amply and fully as was in their power, and ftimulated fome thereby to fuch a degree as to create hope that fome time or other it will produce fruit. Your Honors can inform yourfelves more fully on the fubject by reference to the Reports and Documents fent herewith.

A certain Bifcayan, an inhabitant

of *Caraquas* had, among others, an interview with our Commiffioners and gave them to underftand that he had a new Veffel on the ftocks there with which he was intending at an early day to make a Voyage along the Main from *Caraquas* hitherward, to certain little Iflands lying in the neighborhood of, and oppofite *Bonayre*, near the Main, to catch Turtle, and expected to be engaged there three weeks. It was his intention, according to circum- ftances, to take with him, as a venture, fome Tobacco, Hides and other wares, in order, fhould people come there to trade with him and bring along fuch goods as would be of ufe to him, that he would have payment ready for them, and alfo have a better opportunity to con- verfe about other trade.

With a view, therefore, to encourage thofe people more and more in our favor, I refolved, upon the abovementioned Report, by advice of and after communication with the adjoined Council here, to fend one of the Company's Sloops, with a fmall cargo of fuch things as we could obtain here, as a venture thither. I found faid Bifcayan faithful to his propofal and promife, only he was prevented bringing any Hides or Tobacco with him, by being obliged, by the Governor of *Caraquas*, to convey fome perfons for the King to *Porto Cabelho*, and in order not to create any evil fufpicion in their minds, he dared not on this occafion bring any thing with him in his Bark except a little rough Copper or *Slacken* which he exchanged for the fmall cargo he befpoke from our people, and further made a Propofal and even wrote a Letter to me with his own hand, the original whereof is annexed, to purchafe the Company's Negroes, that is, all that are here at prefent, on the following conditions, to wit; That the Company fhall have a Ship with their own Crew here ready for the Negroes to embark in, and when refolved to accept his offer, to let him know by thofe recently with him, at the place defignated by him, when he will without lofs of time, repair in perfon to this harbor, and enter into an Agreement and terms for what articles and at what price the Negroes fhall be delivered at the place where he hopes to bring them in fafety and without danger; and that he will not receive any Negroes before payment for them fhall be made on board the Ship, and he or his partner fhall remain on board the Ship, with the Negroes until the Conditions and Agreement which will be made here, ſhall be fully carried out.

He reports that the place to which he ſays he will convey them is on the North ſide of *Cuba*, where the (Spaniſh) Nation has no Fortreſs nor means to prevent the project or to diſturb them; alſo that he will leave his own Couſin, who is likewiſe related to the friends to whom he will convey the Negroes, here at *Curaçao* as a Hoſtage and ſecurity, until it be manifeſt that he ſhall have performed in good faith all he has promiſed; as more fully appears by the annexed Relation and report of Cornet *Balthazar Van Eſs* and *Johan Rombouts* on the ſubject. He has requeſted an anſwer to this, for his information. I therefore wiſh your Honors' early

Inſtructions hereupon, as to what I
ſhall do, or omit in this matter, and
that in the meanwhile I may receive a ſupply of proviſions ſufficient
for the Negroes to enable me to
wait for him.

※　　※　　※　　※　　※

I have received the Agreement
and Condition which Your Honors
have concluded with Mr. *Henricus
Matthias*, merchant of *Amſterdam*,
reſpecting the Negroes. On look-
ing and reading it over, I find it
very favorable for that gentleman,
wherefore my impreſſion is that
your Honors' intention in con-
cluding it is to begin and introduce
the trade here. I ſhall not be
wanting, God willing, in obeying
and executing your Honors' orders and Inſtructions in this regard
faithfully and to my beſt ability.
Meanwhile, ſhould it happen that
Q

Mr. *Henricus Matthias's* expected Ship did not arrive here, as it has not yet done, I shall expect your further order and answer whether we shall dare to proceed or not with the Negroes on the aforesaid Biscayan's presented proposals extended as above. In the strong hope and expectation that we shall be able to open a trade with our nearest neighbors, I shall purchase on your Honors' account a small cargo from Skipper *Simon Corneliffen Gilde*, so that they may at least find something on coming here; and our Vessels on passing near *Bonayre* may advise the Biscayan and the other Inhabitant already mentioned, what goods can be purchased here on arriving, taking a sample along to show them, should occasion present, and, at the same time, inform the Biscayan that

I have not received any orders to allow Negroes to leave the Iſland until payment for them has been made, and that I ſhall let him have, within four months after date, a fuller and more explicit anſwer which I hope I ſhall receive from your Honors in the meantime.

I am confident that on theſe Conditions he would readily give *Two hundred* pieces of Eight for a merchantable Negro or Negreſs, one with another, whilſt he gave us to underſtand, that the price of Hides would be *Eighteen* ſhillings.

Vice Director BECK to the Directors at Amsterdam.

Curaçao, 28. July, 1657.

Gentlemen.

✳   ✳   ✳   ✳   ✳

AS I advised your Honors in my last, I dispatched the Freight-boat to the appointed and prefixed place—a certain small Island near the Main—to the Biscayan and sent him word on the subject of his trading for Negroes, as I had informed your Honors more at large in my last. Whereupon he resolved to visit this place in person, in our aforesaid Freight-boat (*Stygerschuit*). He was accompanied by a certain *Padre*, named Friar *Francis* to purchase a few parcels of merchandize with one or two little Negro Girls.

I alfo fold to the abovenamed Bifcayan, a fmall Negro Boy with a few goods, for which he had brought with him fome Hides and Tobacco in our aforefaid Boat ; thefe are fent herewith as a fpecimen by the Ship *Oftrich*, the price of the Hides being *Fifteen* fhillings each and of the Tobacco *Six* pieces of Eight the Arobe of *Twenty five* Pounds. I have fold to the aforefaid *Padre* Friar *Francis*, goods to the amount of *Four hundred* pieces of Eight and *two* little Negro Girls, all at a fair and reafonable price, in order to encourage and ftimulate them to come to thefe Ports to trade, which I think is greatly for the Company's intereft. Wherefore, I let the *Padre* have the *two* little Negro Girls @ *One hundred* and *fifty* pieces of Eight each, which together amounts to *Three hundred* pieces of Eight, and to the aforesaid Biscayan a little Boy @ *One hundred* and *twenty* pieces of Eight. The Merchandizes which I sold them were purchased from the bearer hereof, *Simon Corneliſſen Gilde*, Skipper of the Ship *Oſtrich*, expreſſly for this purpoſe on your Honors' account before their arrival, in order that our neareſt Neighbors on coming here may at leaſt on ſuch occaſion find ſomething for the aſking, until your Honors might ſend ſuch cargoes as the caſe requires, as I have partly explained in my laſt.

Although the abovementioned *Padre*, Friar *Francis*, did not bring with him any payment for what he purchaſed, yet could I not let him go away empty handed, as it was the firſt time, in conſequence of the converſation and verbal Agreement entered into with our Commiſſary and Skipper of the Freight-boat before his arrival here — that is, to let them return to the appointed place with what they had purchafed, on condition that they fhould not land, much lefs receive poffeffion of what has not been paid for here, until they have made payment therefor to the Commiffary and Skipper of the aforefaid freight Boat, in good and fufficient Hides.

   *   *   *   *   *

With regard to the trade in Negroes, the aforefaid Bifcayan, now here, hath given me fuch explanations and further information on that point, that we can come to no other conclufion than that a good and favorable refult is to be expected from it. He hath communicated to me the moft direct and fhorteft route, how and in what manner not only a fhipload of

Negroes, but fucceffively a cargo of good faleable Merchandize befides could be traded off. Were a Ship with neceffaries in the harbor here, he is willing on receiving notice thereof at the appointed place, to come here and enter into fuch agreement with the Company from which as he firmly believes, he and the Company would derive great advantage.

The place the Negroes fhould be conveyed to is called *Porto Velo*, the ftaple place of trade. Permiffion can be obtained to difpofe of the cargo freely there on paying *One hundred* and *thirteen* pieces of Eight for each Negro, which is the Royalty. But fuch permiffion is not given except to perfons of their own Nation; but it can be obtained under the pretext that they had chartered a Dutch Ship and

Crew to fetch and bring over the Negroes, and that the Negroes and Merchandize in the Ship are the property of their Nation.

Such is the manner in which the aforefaid Bifcayan would contract for and purchafe Negroes from the Company on the following Conditions: That he, or his companion, with five or fix more of their Nation, fhall embark at their own expenfe with the Company's Skipper, Commiffary, Crew and Matroffes in the Ship lying ready to fail and profecute with them their Voyage to *Porto Velo*, and after receiving a permit there from the Governor, fell the Negroes which they know they can fell immediately after their arrival at fuch a high price that the outlay of the aforefaid Royalty in order to obtain the Permit, may be eafily repaid. Therefore, they will undertake this themselves, and pay to the Company, after safe arrival there, for each Negro and Negress between *Eighteen* and *thirty* years of age, *Two hundred* Reals or Pieces of Eight, in Silver bars or pieces of Eight; further they will be able to obtain there a proper permit to trade then to other places, to load the Ship with such cargo and freight as the countries supply and are most profitable to the country. In like manner, the price for the Goods being agreed upon and arranged here, the payment there for them shall be made in the same manner as for the Negroes, but the risk of the Sea and the expenses of the Negroes, until they arrive at the above place, must be borne by the Company, but when arrived there, they will be responsible for them. For the full performance of the Conditions which shall be made here on the part of the Company, the aforesaid Biscayan offers to stake his life, and even to remain here in person in the Fort, or to leave another responsible person here in custody of the Company at the risk of his life, if any fraud is, or has been intended or designed. And it is further conditioned that the Negroes in their minority, as well as old and deformed ones, must be disposed of at a special and lower price. On these terms he is resolved, at all times from now henceforth, whenever a Ship with Negroes will be ready here, at the time and place to be named where advice is to be sent him, to come hither and with God's merciful help faithfully to perform whatever is abovementioned.

The other Plan or proposal mentioned in my last, to run the Negroes in at the north fide of *Cuba*, is not, he fays, fo feafible as this.

❋   ❋   ❋   ❋   ❋

Charter of the Ship Eyckenboom for a Voyage to Africa and New Netherland.

IN the Name of the Lord, Amen. In the year of the birth of Our Lord and Saviour *Jefus Chrift*, 1659, the 25th of *January*, before me *Henrick Schaeff*, admitted by the Court of *Holland* a Notary Public refiding in *Amfterdam*, and the underfigned witneffes, in their own perfons came and appeared Meffieurs *Edward Man* and *Abraham Wilmerdoncx*, Directors of the Incorporated Weft India Company at the Chamber here in *Amfterdam* hereunto authorized by the Board of their Affociates, as charterers on the one part, and Skipper *Jan Janfen Eyckenboom* of *Hoorn*, Mafter under God, of his Ship named the *Eyckenboom*, long 1^{c}xx, wide xxv and one half, hold xi and one half, over it five and one half and fix feet, with a half deck and forecaftle on either fide, and the aforefaid parties declared and do hereby declare to have made and concluded together a certain Contract for a charter of faid Ship, in the form and manner hereinafter defcribed, To wit:

That the aforefaid Skipper fhall be bound immediately to deliver his aforefaid Ship here in the City fitted out, tight, well caulked, and provided with good and fufficient anchors, cordage, tackle, fails, running and ftanding rigging and all other neceffaries and appurtenances thereunto belonging, and the fame to mount with *Ten* good pieces of Cannon, with the requifite powder and fhot 'and other ammunition in proportion, but the neceffary confumption of powder and fhot aforefaid fhall be made good by the Company, which fhall alfo put on board faid Ship in addition to the *Ten* pieces aforefaid as many other guns as they pleafe and can conveniently place, and fhall provide and pay the expence of the powder and fhot therefor, on condition that in the neceffary confumption thereof, the aforefaid Skipper fhall bear the contingent of his Ship aforefaid; that further, faid Company fhall man faid Ship with fuch and fo many hands and provide them with fuch ftores as faid Company will pleafe and think proper. Which being done on the one fide and the other, the aforefaid Ship fhall on the part of faid Company, be laden with a full and fuitable cargo, or to fuch extent as faid Company fhall think proper; being laden with all fuch goods, wares and merchandizes as they will determine, the aforefaid Ship fhall, with the firft fair wind and weather that God will grant, be difpatched and fail from this country direct to the Coaft of *Africa* and run along faid Coaft from above downward, or from *Cape Verd* down, and touch, trade, lie and remain at all trading pofts and ports, according to the pleafure of faid Company and their Commiffary, unto the Caftle *St. George d'el Mina*, where they fhall receive or find orders from the Company's Director General and Council or fhall be furnifhed with them on failing hence; And fail towards the Bight of *Guinea* and touch and trade at all other places lying therein according to the order which shall be given him by the Director General or here; from thence proceed further to the Islands of *Curaçao, Bonaire,* and *Aruba* in the *West Indies,* and also to *New Netherland,* and all round every where else the Company, or its Ministers, shall determine and order, and likewise at all said quarters and places trade and traffic Goods, Wares and Merchandizes and also take in people, load and unload at the pleasure of the aforesaid Company or its Ministers; And to that end sail to and from, run hither and thither, anchor, lie, load and unload at said Coasts, Quarters and Places as often and as frequently and so long as the service of the Company such shall demand; Furthermore, return and come thence to this city *Amfterdam* or the deftined port of difcharge, and on her fafe return and arrival, there difcharge and deliver to the aforefaid Company her laden return cargo and goods. Which done, there fhall be paid to him the Skipper for the contracted freight, every month, the fum of *Eight hundred* guilders of xx ftivers each, on condition that the Company is bound for the term of *Six* fucceffive months or longer, to be calculated according to the length of time, all current months according to the Almanac, to run and commence when the Ship fhall, in the profecution of the Voyage, reach the Sea outfide the laft buoy of the *Texel*, and to expire when fhe fhall arrive and caft anchor before this city of *Amfterdam* or her deftined port of discharge, payable xiiii days @ three weeks after the aforesaid discharge here, besides average and pilotage according to the custom of the Sea, and over and above also Hat money for the abovenamed Skipper at the Company's discretion. And said Skipper, with and besides the Company's Crew, shall also make the Voyage with the aforesaid Ship in order to look to said Ship, her appurtenances, &c., making use of the Company's stores, but the monthly pay or wages not being at its charge; And he shall be, over and above, subject to the orders and instructions, articles and other rules of the Company during the Voyage, no more nor less than if he had been sworn to observe the same, they being taken as inserted herein, and especially also in regard to particular or private forbidden trading, in shipping or conveyance of particular or private goods, merchandizes or wares, on pain according to the aforesaid Articles, Orders and Instructions of the said Company. The abovementioned Directors, parties hereunto, pledging for the payment of the aforesaid contracted monthly or freight moneys, average and pilotage, their private persons and property, and the aforesaid Skipper, specially, also his person, Ship, appurtenances and contracted freight moneys, and generally all his other property, real and personal, present and to come without any exception, submitting the same to the Court of *Holland* and all laws and judges, all aboveboard. Done at *Amsterdam* in the presence of *Cryn van Seventer* and *Marten Hegervelt*, free citizens (*poorters*) here, witnesses hereunto invited.

Bill of Lading of Negroes.

I, *Jan Pieterfen* of *Dockum*, Skipper under God of my Ship named the *Spera Mundi*, now lying ready before *Curaçao*, with the firſt fair wind which God ſhall vouchſafe, to ſail to *New Netherland*, where my correct unloading ſhall take place, acknowledge that I have received under the deck of my aforeſaid Ship, from you *Frans Bruyn*, to wit, *Five* Negroes, whereof one is a Negreſs, all dry and well conditioned, and marked with the annexed mark. All which I promiſe to deliver (if God grant me a ſafe Voyage) with my aforeſaid Ship at *N. Netherland* aforeſaid, to the Honble Director General *Petrus Stuyveſant*, or his Factor or Deputies, on payment for the freight of the above defcribed goods, at the difcretion of the faid Director General, and for the performance hereof, I bind myfelf, and all my goods and my aforefaid Ship and appurtenances. In witnefs of the truth, I have figned three Copies hereof with my name, all of the fame tenor, the one being fatisfied, the others to be void. Written at *Curaçao* the 24th day of *Auguft*, Anno 1659.

JAN PIETERS GROS
of *Dockum*.

Vice Director BECK to Director STUYVESANT.

Curaçao, Auguſt, 1659.

Honorable, Valiant, Wife, Prudent and moſt Diſcreet Sir.

Sir,

I NOW tranſmit to your Honor duplicates of what I have already ſent by the Galiot *New Amſtel*, Skipper *Auguſtinus Heermans*, and it will be very agreeable to me if I may be informed by the earlieſt opportunity of their ſpeedy and ſafe arrival. I would not forego the preſent favorable occaſion and opportunity of the Ship *Spera Mundi*, *Jan Pieterſen* Skipper, to acquaint you of the circumſtances of this Iſland up to the preſent time (God be praifed!) in regard to the Commerce with our neareft Neighbors. Hitherto there have not been imported as many goods as the demand requires, and efpecially the trade in Negroes at this place which the Company hath referved to itfelf, or elfe all are fold.

There are lying here, at prefent, two Ships ready to fail hence for Fatherland, which occupy my whole time, fo that I have not much leifure to write to your Honor at length. The one is the Company's Ship called the *King Solomon*, which arrived here on the 2d of July from *Guinea*, with *Three hundred* and *thirty one* Slaves. Of thefe I have fold 300 @ *One hundred* and *fifty* pieces of Eight each, to a certain Spanifh trader whom I am daily expecting to come here and receive them, which I wifh may occur before the departure of the aforefaid two Ships in order to be able to tranfmit the proceeds to the Lords Mafters.

Franck Bruyn purchafed out of the aforefaid lot of Negroes for your Honor, *Two* Boys and a Girl who go over in this Ship. I have done every thing poffible to protect them againft the cold. *Franck Bruyn* hath alfo purchafed *Two* for Commiffary *Van Brugh*, who likewife go by this conveyance on faid Commiffary's account. Your Honor will pleafe to have fuch payment collected therefor from faid *Van Brugh* for the Company, as you will confider juft. Commiffary *Laurens van Ruyven* hath alfo purchafed *Two* young Negroes here for account of his brother the Secretary of your Province, at the fame price as the lot fold for here, viz., *One* *hundred* and *fifty* Patacoons.* I am ſtill in daily expectation of a Ship with Negroes. I wiſh they were come, even were they a thouſand head. I expect the abovementioned merchant here, as already ſtated, to take away thoſe of the *King Solomon.* He is well able and will eagerly buy the whole lot at once.

I have received orders from the Lords Maſters to ſend your Honor againſt the Spring, ſome *fifteen or ſixteen* Negroes whom I could have eaſily diſpatched now, but we have no coarſe cloth to clothe them, and are fearful that they will not be able to endure the Winter there. As Negroes will be plenty here in future, I thought it beſt, according to orders, to poſtpone ſending them

---

* A Spaniſh Coin of the Value of $1.04.

T

until the Spring, when I shall be sending a young Negro Girl for Mr. *Augustinus Heermans* according to his request. Meanwhile, I hope to receive for my instruction, your Honor's advice and order as to whether you will require any more Negroes than the above, and of what age and in what numbers you wish them sent.

* * * * *

1659. December 26, Director *Stuyvesant* writing to the Directors at *Holland* says:

"The Negroes purchased at *Curaçao* for *fl* 140 @ 150 and paid for, cannot be sold here (at *New Amsterdam*) again at that price, either in Beaver or Tobacco, so that all the expences of going and returning are entirely lost."

Vice Director BECK *to the Directors of the Weft India Company.*

Curaçao, 4*th Feb.*, 1660.

Noble, Honorable, Refpected, Wife, Prudent and moft Difcreet Gentlemen.

Gentlemen,

MY laft to your Honors, dated 5. January, as per copy enclofed, was by the Ship *Gideon*, Skipper *Simon Corneliffen* by way of the *Caribbean Iflands*.

* * * * *

You will learn from my laft letters, and from the annexed papers fent again herewith, the fate of the Ship *St. John*, which was due here from *Guinea* with Negroes, and which according to your Honors' orders was to replace the Ship *Diemen* here. What caufes us moſt grief here is, that your Honors have thereby loſt ſuch a fine lot of Negroes and ſuch a faſt ſailing Bark which has been our right arm here.*

Although I have ſtrained every nerve to overtake the Robbers of the Negroes and Bark, as ſtated in my laſt, yet have I not been as ſuccefsful as I wiſhed. I ſhall communicate the particulars to your Honors, God willing, by the Ship *St. George*, which is about to ſail direct from hence this month. If no remedy can be found to prevent ſuch Robberies, and villainous crimes as the carrying away of the Company's Slaves and Bark, and no proſecution and redreſs follow, they will not

---

* See Journal and Papers in firſt Part of this Volume.

only perfift therein, but even ftrike terror into the Spanifh merchants who come here to trade.

Inclofed herein goes a Minute of what I have provifionally judged neceffary, with the advice of the Council, to be done againft them. Copy thereof has been furnifhed to *Simon Corneliffe Gilde*, to be ufed by him, according to circumftances. And although my zeal be hearty and fincere to purfue fuch Robbers, and as much as poffible, to repair and make good your Honors' loffes, yet have I been fcrupulous, as I did not wifh to do too much or too little. Therefore do I refpectfully folicit your Honors to fupply me herein with fuch orders, ample advice and power, that I may fet to work and execute them unfcrupuloufly againft fimilar and fuch like Robbers, when occafion offers, so that others may take example therefrom. Had we had here a faſt ſailing Yacht of fourteen guns, manned in proportion, we might, without doubt, have overtaken and again recovered by force or with good right, the aforeſaid Negroes and Bark, and it grieves us that we for want thereof could not carry out our good intentions.

We regret exceedingly that ſuch Rovers ſhould have been the cauſe of the ill ſucceſs of the zeal we feel to attract the Spaniſh traders hither for your Honors' benefit, by previous notices and otherwiſe, for the augmentation of Commerce and the ſale of the Negroes which are to come here more and more in your Honors' Ships and for your account. What is lawfully done by Engliſh Ships with regular orders and Commiſſion againſt their Enemies, even the Spanish Nation, and not against us, we must tolerate; but when most of the damage is inflicted without lawful order and Commission, not only on the Spanish Nation, but even on ourselves, it ought not to be tolerated, and should, by all ways and means, be driven from the Sea.

I have witnessed with pleasure your Honors' diligence in providing us here from time to time with Negroes. That will be the only bait to allure hither the Spanish Nation, as well from the Main as from other parts, to carry on trade of any importance. But the more subtly and quietly the trade to and on this Island can be carried on, the better will it be for this place and yours.

※ ※ ※ ※ ※

Inasmuch as Mr. *Gysbert de Rosa*, who is with me, is authorized by the private persons interested in the Ship *Hope* to apply to the Governor of the *Havana*, by whom we understand the Rover has been arrested, and to that end have sent to me such papers, letters and proofs as may serve for the recovery of said Ship and cargo, nevertheless up to this time have we had no opportunity to effect the work according to our good inclination, except that Mr. *Gysbert de Roosa* has recently sent his Yacht, *The Young St. Paul*, with a cargo to *St. Jago de Cuba*, by which we wrote conjointly a letter to the Governor at *Havanna* to be sent to him overland from *Cuba*, to give said Governor some premonition, until a more favorable opportunity shall present itself to carry out your Honors' intentions and thofe of the private friends who are interefted.

I firft received the contract entered into by your Honors with Meff^{rs} *Hector Pieterfen* and *Guillaume Momma*, by the Ships *Gideon* and *Love*, after the Negroes that had come by the Ship *King Solomon* had all been fold, and although the Ship *Eyckenboom* has not yet arrived, two Spanifh Veffels with a Yacht from *Cadiz* have caft anchor in this port on the 2d January. They are come purfuant to exprefs orders to the Captain of the aforefaid Veffel *Pedro Sorilho* by name, for the purpofe of taking away thofe Negroes, according to contract; and Skipper *Ewout Janfen* has exhibited thofe orders to me, and this gave me to underftand, that in cafe they fhould leave here without Negroes, the whole object of their Voyage would be thereby fruſtrated, and they ſhould in conſequence ſuffer exceſſive damages. I found myſelf, therefore, obliged to ſolicit as well the freemen as the Company's ſervants, to loan from their Plantations to the Company as many Negroes as they could poſſibly ſpare, under the promiſe that good ſtout Negroes ſhould be returned in their ſtead, out of the firſt lot which would come for the Company. In this way, what with the *Cape Verde* Negroes, and thoſe of the Company and of private individuals, I have collected together with great trouble *Sixty two* head. As there were among them ſome old and ſome young, *two* were deducted for them, as appears by the original Receipt tranſmitted herewith. They have accordingly paid me here for *Forty ſix* head, as per contract, @ *One hundred* and *twenty* pieces of Eight, amounting to *Five thousand, five hundred* and *twenty* pieces of Eight, leaving *Fourteen* head of Negroes, for which the aforesaid Messrs *Hector Pieterſen* and *Guillaume Momma* are to pay your Honors in *Holland*, as is more fully set forth in the receipt to which for brevity sake I refer.

* * * * *

The aforesaid Captain, highly gratified and contented, sailed from here with his two Ships on the 15th January for *Porto Bello*, as he informed me.

* * * * *

I received by the Ship *Gideon*, from *Cape Verde* only *Twenty eight* Slaves, old and young, as appears by the receipt delivered to the Skipper. In consequence of their condition and age, they are not worth so much as the Negroes lately brought by the *King Solomon*. But I have since been informed that if a handsome lot of Negroes could, when opportunity offers, be imported from that place, those would proportionably advance in price.

What your Honors recommend to me in regard to Privateers, that they shall not be allowed to come here or hereabouts, I have fully communicated to our opposite Neighbors,* and to the Spanish Nation in other places. Few Privateers will come into our harbor, because they know that they are suspected here, unless they come into port in numbers under one pretence or another, to see if they cannot obtain some advantage over us for purposes of plunder, as the Rovers

---

* That is in *Venezuela* and the Spanish Main. ED.

have indeed threatened us. Though well on our guard here againſt them, yet muſt our defence depend on human hands in ſuch circumſtances. The reinforcement your Honors have now ſent in the Ship *Love* is not ſufficient to oppoſe a great force, becauſe, on the other hand, as many of the old Soldiers, whoſe time is expired, are going away as nearly balance the reinforcement juſt arrived.

With ſo few men we cannot reſiſt any evil diſpoſed Spaniards, if they ſhould have any bad deſign in their heads, and be as ſtrong as the two Ships which lately arrived here in our Harbor with full *Two hundred* and *fifty* hands. The ſame holds good in regard to the French and Engliſh Privateers, who heretofore have viſited our Harbor, and we place as little confidence in the one as in the other. The Spaniards feeing that we are fo weak, can get up one pretext or another, efpecially thofe who come from *Spain*, who look on this trade with a jealous eye. For, fome Merchants who arrived in this port with the aforefaid two Ships, have, as I am informed, alleged here to one and another, that the Trade which we carry on here with the Spanifh Nation on the Coaft or elfewhere, would not be permitted in *Spain*, and fuch a prohibition would be iffued that no Spaniard belonging to any place would dare to come hither for the purpofe of trade. On the other hand, I have underftood from the Captain himfelf, that they are confident the Trade here will flourifh more and more, and he hoped that his Ship, the *St. Catharine*, would return here in four months with *Three* to *Four thoufand* pieces of Eight to purchafe Negroes and Merchandize. This was confirmed to me by the Dutch Skipper *Ewout Janfen*, in cafe they arrive fafe at *Porto Bello*. The Spanifh Frigates which have been previoufly here, and trade to *New Spain*, have alfo told me the fame thing, and faid that they came yearly from *New Spain* up to *Caraccas*, with confiderable cafh to trade there for Cocoa and Merchandize, and that they then would feek a pretext to touch, on their way from *Caraccas*, here to purchafe Negroes and ftock goods.

Receipt of PEDRO DIEZ TROX-XILLA *for Slaves.*

I, UNDERWRITTEN, hereby acknowledge to have received from the Honble *Mathias Beck*, Governor over the *Curaçao* Iflands, *Sixty two* Slaves, old and young, in fulfillment and performance of the Contract concluded on the 26th June, A° 1659, by Meff^rs *Hector Pieters* and *Guilliamme Momma*, with the Lords Directors at the Chamber at *Amfterdam*; and as the Negroes by the Ship *King Solomon*, were difpofed of, long before the arrival of the underfigned, and the Ship *Eyckenboom*, mentioned in the aforefaid Contract, has not arrived at this date, the faid Governor has furnifhed me, the underfigned, with the abovementioned *Sixty two*

Slaves, and on account of the old and young which are among the aforefaid Negroes, has allowed a deduction of *two* Negroes, fo that there remain *Sixty* head in the clear, for which I, the underfigned, have here according to Contract, paid to the Governor aforefaid for *Forty fix* head, (*a One hundred* and *twenty* pieces of Eight, amounting to *Five thoufand, five hundred* and *twenty* pieces of Eight. Whereas, *Fourteen* Negroes remain ftill to be paid for, according to Contract in *Holland* by Meff[rs] *Hector Pieters* and *Guillame Momma* in *Amflerdam*, to Meff[rs] the Directors aforefaid, on prefentation of this my receipt, to which end three of the fame tenor are executed and figned in the prefence of two underfigned truft-worthy witneffes, whereof the one being fatisfied the others are to be

W

void. *Curaçao* in Fort *Amſterdam*, the 11th *January*, A° 1660. It being underſtood that the above *Fourteen* Negroes, to be paid for in *Amſterdam*, ſhall not be charged higher than according to Contract @ *Two hundred* and *eighty* Guilders each, amounting together to *Three thouſand, nine hundred* and *twenty* Carolus Guilders. Dated as above.

  Pedro Diez Troxxilla,
  Ewout Jansen.

Witneſſes,
 Nicolaes Haeck,
 L. V. Ruyven.

Director STUYVESANT *to Vice Director* BECK.

Amsterdam in *New Netherland,*
17 *February,* 1660.

* * * * *

FOUR Negro Boys and *one* Negro Girl have, as you advised, been sent to, and received by me ⅌ the Ship *Sphera Mundi;* 3 on mine and 2 on Commissary *Van Brugge*'s account, their price being left to our discretion. Upon this subject I must say, that the assignment sent to me by *Frans Bruyn* is unsigned. However, in order to avoid any difficulty, I left this time the choice to the Commissary who took the Negro Girl and one of the stoutest Boys. But greater difficulties have arisen in this wise:

One of the *Five* died on the paffage hither; fome were fick or have become fo after arriving. To prevent any mifunderftanding in future, the fold Negroes ought to be configned to the purchafer by their names or marks.

As regards the price which was left to our difcretion, in order to prevent any fufpicion of felf intereftednefs, I wifh your Honor to inform me after the others have been fold, what price they brought.

I have obferved by your defpatch to the Honble Directors, dated 3 *September*, forwarded by the Ship *Sphera Mundi* the 26 December laft, that the Negroes were fold to Mr *Corn^s van Ool* @ 140 pieces of Eight, viz., from 40 to 16 years; from 16 to 12 years, three for two; under 12 years, two for one.

We hope and truft that by complying with such price and terms, we shall avoid all suspicion of self interest. I am willing to take my share of the expence and risk of their passage hither, because I desired the Negroes for my own service and the promotion of Agriculture, not in the expectation of any gain, and therefore sent for young ones, in which regard the worthy Inhabitants, Christians, and those of the Honble Company, ought, I think, to be preferred before Spaniards and unbelieving Jews.

You will see by the enclosed extracts from my letter covering yours to the Honble Directors, what I have proposed to them. It is therefore desirable and somewhat necessary that a fixed price should be set on Horses conveyed hither, or ordered from *Curaçao*, by private persons, as well as on Negroes as far as practicable, according to their ability and age, becaufe the one as well as the other are moft urgently required here for purpofes of Agriculture and its advancement, and finally would tend to the greater advantage, trade and profperity of the Honble Company and its fubjects.

* * * * *

In regard to the Negroes which the Honble Directors ordered to be fent hither, they ought to be ftout and ftrong fellows, fit for immediate employment on this Fortrefs and other works; alfo, if required, in war againft the Wild Barbarians, either to purfue them when retreating, or elfe to carry fome of the Soldiers' baggage; it being very apparent that we fhall be conftrained to wage a righteous and offenfive War againft them, for the peaceable poffeffion once of the Land, and the avenging of numerous fuffered affronts and murders. An important fervice would be conferred on the Company, on us and the Country if there were among the fold Negroes, fome of experience who had refided a certain time at *Curaçao*.

Directors at Amfterdam to Director STUYVESANT.

Amfterdam, the 9th March, 1660.

* * * * *

NOW as regards the trade in Slaves, or Negroes, which the Inhabitants there at *Curaçao* might purfue, that is permitted to them as to other Merchants, with the underftanding, however, that it is not to be at a lower price, for the reaſon that the Company here would thereby be ſerioufly prejudiced. But as Agriculture there would be beneficially promoted by Negroes, and the advancement thereof is of great importance, and the profperity of that State is, for the moſt part, dependent thereon, we have, therefore, concluded and even refolved to try an experiment with a parcel of Negroes which we ſhall have conveyed to your Honor by the firſt opportunity which a Ship or Ships may offer from *Curaçao*. Theſe Negroes ſhall then be publicly fold to the higheſt bidder there, on the exprefs Condition, neverthelefs, that they ſhall not be removed thence, but be employed in cultivating the Land. To this end, an exact regiſter ſhall be made and kept, as your Honor will fee by the accompanying form of the aforefaid Conditions.

※ ※ ※ ※ ※

Propofed Contract to import Slaves into New Netherland.

THIS day, the underfigned Director and Council of *New Netherland*, thereunto authorized by Refolution of the Chamber at *Amfterdam*, on the one part, and the Owners of the Ship whereof   is Skipper, burthen about   Tons, on the other part, have agreed and contracted that a Permit and Commiffion in due form fhall be granted to the aforefaid Skipper, to buy Slaves, and further to profecute fuch advantage as faid Owners fhall deem expedient on the Coast of *Africa*; in like manner to return here to the *Manhattans* with the said Slaves and their further cargo, provided neverthelefs that they shall not be at liberty, in regard to the Coast of *Africa*, to refort on the granted Permit to the *Gold Coast*, and therefore not to go Westerly further than *Ardre* or at most to *Popo*, on pain of the lofs of the Ship and Goods laden therein, to which end the Directors and Council shall be at liberty to place a Supercargo on board said Ship, (whom the Skipper shall be bound to entertain in the Cabin,) and if neceffary to caufe the People therein to be fworn; for which aforefaid Permit and Commiffion the aforefaid Owners promife, on the return of the said Ship and before her difcharge, promptly to pay to the Director and Council aforefaid, or their deputies, a duty of *Fifteen* Guilders for each Negro, without making any exception or objection thereto. Under bond of their perfons and Goods, none excepted, with renunciation of benefit *ordinis divifionis et excuffionis*, having entire knowledge thereof. Done *New Amfterdam* this

Remonftrance on the preceding propofed Contract.

Honorable, Wife, Prudent Lords, *Petrus Stuyvefant*, Governor General, and the Councillors of *New Netherland, Curaçao* and Dependencies thereof.

Honorable,

THE Underfigned Burghers and Inhabitants of this City *New Amfterdam,* your Honors' liege Subjects, moſt reſpectfully repreſent that they are inclined to a foreign Trade, and eſpecially to the Coaſt of *Africa*, according to the Conceſſion of the Honble Directors granted in the year 1652, as a ſpecial privilege to the Inhabitants of this Place, in order to fetch thence Slaves and other Wares might be diſpoſed of here and elſewhere, whereby this City and the entire Country would increaſe and proſper in Merchandize, Commerce, Population and more eſpecially in the Tobacco Trade, to the advantage not only of theſe Inhabitants, but alſo of the Hon[ble] Weſt India Company which would behold, in time, a vaſt, populous, and rich commercial Province ſpring up in theſe parts therefrom.

But it has appeared to them that thoſe who would execute with

Skipper or Merchant going to that Country a Draft of Partnerſhip, which is beſet and pinched by ſuch preciſe Conditions, would riſk their lives and Goods, and at beſt gain nothing, or run the riſk of having Ship and Goods confiſcated. For, beſides the entire of the *Gold Coaſt* being excepted in that Conceſſion, it appears that *Cape Verde, Siera Leona,* the *Greyn* (Pepper) and *Qua Qua* Coaſt are alſo excluded; for it is not permitted to reſort further Weſt, at fartheſt, than *Popo Sonde.* Moreover, the *Gold Coaſt* which from *Cape Apolonia* to *Cape des Rodes* or *Mount Berique* is reckoned 60 leagues, can be extended much further, as will be ſeen, to any place where Gold may be found. And as regards Slaves; for each head 15 Guilders muſt be paid, and then the payment for them in Tobacco or Beaver, is again taxed when shipped to Fatherland, which imposes too heavy a burthen on this hazardous Trade.

The Honble Company, in the meanwhile, must perceive that our Neighbors the French, English, Swedes, Danes and Courlanders, are by means of the Netherlanders who repair to them, trading along the entire Coast, even under their strongholds, without any profit being derived therefrom by the Company; Yea, they suffer rather very serious loss thereby, as is manifest from the example of *Arent de Groot* who in the Year 1638, built a Fort at *Cormantyn* for the English, and of *Hendrick Caerloff*, the former Fiscal, who built another at *Cape Corse* in the Year 1650, for the Swedes.

Your Honors' subjects passing by these strongholds, take another course and as faithful subjects, address themselves to you, humbly praying permission to trade free and unobstructed in Ship or Ships, along the whole of the West Coast of *Africa*, that is, from *Cape Verd* to *Cape Lopes de Gonsalve*, in all Bays, Rivers and Coasts, without any exception, the Hon[ble] Company's strongholds alone excepted, according to the Rules and Orders, on payment, either here or in *Holland*, of such moderate duty as shall be agreed on. This doing, &c.

 (Signed)
   Cornelius Steenwyck,
   Marten Kregier,
   Themotheus Gabrie,
   Oloff Stevensen,
   Govert Loocquermans,
   Jacob Strycker.
   P. L. Vande Grift,
   Pieter Rudolphus,
   Hendrick Jansen Vander Vier,
   Peter Couwenhoven,
   Jacob Steendam,
   Johannes Verveelen.

The preceding Petition being read and confidered, the following Apoftil was annexed thereto:

The Director General and Council confider themfelves unqualified, without the previous knowledge and approbation of their Superiors, the Lords Directors of the Incorporated Weft India Company, Chamber at *Amfterdam*, to grant any further enlargement than the Act herein mentioned implies. The Petitioners, therefore, muft make application on the fubject to that Board. Done *Fort Amfterdam* in *New Netherland*, 3d May, 1660.

Bill of Lading of Negroes.

I UNDERWRITTEN *Jan Janfen Eyckenboom*, Skipper under God of my Ship called the *Eyck-*

enboom, lying at prefent in the Harbor of the Ifland of *Curaçao*, ready to fail for *New Netherland*, hereby acknowledge to have received in my Ship aforefaid from the Hon^(ble) Vice Director *Matthias Beck* for account of the Hon^(ble) Company, *Twenty* head of Sound Slaves or Male Negroes, whom I undertake and promife to deliver after the profperous and fafe arrival of my Ship in *New Netherland*, unto the Hon^(ble) Director General and Council there, firft acknowledging to have executed triplicate . Receipts therefor, one of which being fatisfied, the others fhall be void. *Curaçao* in *Fort Amfterdam*, the 8 *May*, A° 1660.

JAN JANSE EYCKENBOOM.

Director STUYVESANT *to the Directors at Amſterdam.*

Amſterdam in *New Netherland,*
25 *June,* 1660.

* * * * *

WE are this inſtant informed by a Fiſherman, that the Galiot *New Amſtel* is in fight with another flute with Horſes and Negroes from *Curaçao.* We ſhall communicate to your Honors by the firſt opportunity, perhaps the Ship *Faith,* what intelligence we receive from there, and in the mean time will execute your orders as to the ſale of the Negroes.

* * * * *

The Flute already mentioned, which arrived here from *Curaçao* with the Galiot is named the *Eyck-*

enboom, and was difpatched 16 or 17 months ago in the fervice and pay of the Company to *Guinea*, and thence with Negroes to *Curaçao*.

* * * * *

Nineteen Negroes arrived here in the fame Veffel; the twentieth died on the Voyage. The remainder are in tolerable health.

Director STUYVESANT *to Vice Director* BECK.

Amfterdam in *New Netherland,* } 5 *July,* 1660.

* * * * *

IN refpect to the *Three* Negro Boys received by the Ship *Sphera Mundi*, they will be accepted on the fame terms as thofe fo told *Van Olen*. You will pleafe to enter them on our account there, and offset them againſt what has been heretofore delivered out of our *coreal* to the ſtore there.

Nineteen of the 20 head of Negroes which your Honor ſent on the Company's account, have arrived in tolerable condition and health.

 * * * * *

It has pleaſed the Honble Company, on our propoſal tranſmitted by the Ship *Sphera Mundi,* in regard to the trade in Negroes and the equalization of duties between the two Conqueſts, to write, on the firſt, in order to make no alteration to the Company's prejudice in the Negro trade at *Curaçao,* that they had reſolved for the promotion of Agriculture, to ſend thence hither a good number of Negroes, to be ſold to the Inhabitants, on condition that they ſhall not be tranſported elſewhere, believing that, by this method, the Honble Company will suffer lefs lofs and the People reap greater benefit. The effect hereof we fhall leave to time.

Bill of Lading of Negroes.

I, UNDERWRITTEN *Dirck Janfen* from *Oldenburch*, Skipper under God of my Ship named the *New Netherland Indian*, at prefent lying in the Harbor of the Ifland of *Curaçao*, ready to fail to *New Netherland*, hereby acknowledge to have received from the Honble Vice Director *Matthias Beck*, for account of the Honble Company, *Ten* head of Sound Slaves or Male Negroes, whom I undertake and promife to deliver, after my fafe arrival with my Ship in *New Netherland*, to the Honble Director

General and Council there, firſt ſigning three Receipts of the ſame tenor, of which when one is ſatisfied the others are void. *Curaçao,* in Fort Amſterdam, the 31ſt *Auguſt,* A° 1660.

DIERCK JANS.

1661. July 21. A ſimilar Bill of Lading for 40 Slaves, confiſting of 15 Men, 14 Women, 6 Boys and 5 Girls, to be delivered in *New Netherland.*

Permit to export a crazy Negro to Virginia.

THE Petition of *Samuel Edſal,* ſetting forth that one of the Negroes purchaſed by him on the 8th of October laſt at public Auction from the Director General and Council is unfit to perform any fort of work, as he is fometimes not in his right mind, and requefting permiffion to fend him to *Virginia*, being read and confidered, it is Apoftilled—

The Petition is granted on condition that the Petitioner, when opportunity offers, fhall import or caufe to be imported into the Country another in ftead thereof. Done 20th *January*, 1661.

Directors at Amfterdam to Director STUYVESANT.

Amfterdam, 11*th April*, 1661.

Honorable, Prudent, Valiant, Beloved, Faithful.

THE bearer hereof has fafely handed us your Letter of the 9th ultimo, which came by way of New and Old *England*. The Neceſſaries required therein, not already ſent, ſhall be forwarded to you in the Veſſels now lying ready to ſail direct thither.

This goes by way of *Curaçao*. And as we have obſerved by the encloſures thereof, that the greater portion of the Slaves conveyed thither by the *Eyckenboom* and *New Netherland Indian*, have been ſold at a fair price, we have written to Vice Director *Beck* at *Curaçao* herewith, and ordered him to provide you with a freſh ſupply by every opportunity. We have done this the rather, becauſe we have reſolved not only that Slaves ſhall be kept in *New Netherland*, as we have heretofore ordered, but be moreover exported to the Engliſh and other Neighbors. This, however, on condition that on ſuch occafion there fhall be paid, on each exported Negro, a duty of *Two* Beavers, which is a fmall and light impoft.

The reafons which have led us to the adoption of fuch Refolution, are, among others none of the fmalleft, the promotion both of Agriculture and Trade in thofe Parts, as herefrom a greater frequentation of the water communication betwen *New Netherland* and *Curaçao*, muft neceffarily follow, and tend accordingly to their profperity. Thus the one will be fupplied and provided with neceffaries by the other, which is a matter of great confideration in regard to foreign Poffeffions.

As your Honor obferves, our zeal and care for the welfare of *New Netherland*, fo muft you endeavor to retain us therein and confequently not fail to fend us, from time to time, fuch returns as may accrue there from the fale of the Slaves, in which cafe we fhall not neglect to have your Honor fupplied with others by every opportunity.

Herewith,
Honorable, Prudent, Valiant, Beloved, Faithful, commending you to God's protection we remain,
The Directors of the Weft India Company, at the Chamber of *Amfterdam,*
     C. WITSEN,
     EDWARD MAN.

Director Stuyvesant *to Vice Director* Beck.

Honorable, Wife, Prudent, right Difcreet Sir.

YOUR welcome Letter of the 31ft of Auguft of laft Year, was handed to us in due courfe by the Bearer, in which is firft mentioned the unfortunate lofs for the Company on the Horfes fent hither in the Ship *Eyckenboom* and Galiot *New Amftel*. You Honor will learn from the annexed return of the public fale, what they brought here in confequence of their emaciated appearance after having been refrefhed during two or three months.

We have had better luck with the few Slaves fent hither at the fame time. They were fold to the higheft bidder, chiefly at Beaver's value, which differs little from Silver pay. I have retained some of the best for the Company. One with another they brought about *fl.* 440* a head, less the freight.

On this point, we must not neglect to recommend, in case Negroes are hereafter sent in one and the same Vessel, some on the Company's, and others on private account, as happened in the Ship *Indian*, that on such occasions, the Negroes sent for account of the Company, or Individuals, may be distinguished the one from the other by some particular marks or tokens, either by a stripe on the clothing or otherwise, in order to prevent disputes and differences here, which we might easily have had here with the Owners of the Ship *Indian* if any had fallen sick or died on the

* Equal to $176.

paſſage, ſince they claimed to be entitled to the firſt choice, leaving the reſt for the Company. This choice I alſo have allowed them, as there were no certain marks to guide us.   *   *   *   *

Amſterdam in *New Netherland,* }
16*th April,* A° 1661.   }
(By the *New Netherland Indian.*)

Reſolution of the Director and Council of New Netherland.

Friday, 2*d September,* 1661.

IN COUNCIL. Preſent—
The Honorable Director General
Petrus Stuyveſant,
Hon. *Nicaſius de Sille,*
Johan de Decker.

WHEREAS, the Yacht *New Netherland Indian* arrived here yeſterday from *Curaçao,* by which

I have received on the Company's Account 36 out of 40 head of Negroes and Negreſſes, both young and old, that had been ſhipped in that Veſſel, it is reſolved in order to prevent expence and loſs by death or otherwiſe, to ſell them publicly on Tueſday next to the higheſt bidder, and to announce the ſame immediately every where by Notices.

It being taken into conſideration in regard to the above ſubject, what pay the above Negroes ſhould be ſold for, it is by a majority of Votes reſolved, to ſell them for Beaver or Proviſions, ſuch as Beef, Pork, Wheat or Peaſe, at Beaver price; for if they are to be ſold for Beaver or Caſh down, or Tobacco at Beaver price, neither Burgher nor Farmer can purchaſe any, ſince there is no Tobacco, much leſs Beaver in circulation among the People. By this means, a few perſons only, to whom the Company is indebted, would have an opportunity to monopolize them in diminution of the debt, and that at a ſmall price, becauſe, as already ſtated, ſuch only will be for their intereſt, whereby then, the Company will be fruſtrated out of the Beaver or Tobacco down, and we, alſo, ſhall be obliged to purchaſe a quantity of Proviſions for the Garriſon againſt the coming Winter, and in payment thereof take up Goods from the Merchants at the higheſt price, and next year again loſe thereby the greateſt portion of the Beaver. Therefore, for theſe and many other reaſons it has been thought beſt to ſell the aforeſaid Negroes for Beaver or Proviſions at Beaver price.

Director Stuyvesant *to the Directors at Amſterdam.*

Fort *Amſterdam* in *New Netherland*, 31ſt *October*, 1661.

Honorable, &c.

AS nothing of conſequence has tranſpired ſince the departure of the *Faith* and *Gilded Eagle,* by which the condition of affairs had been explained at large, and nothing of any importance has ſince occurred, this Letter is principally intended to accompany Invoices, Muſter Rolls of the Garriſon, and a few neceſſary Documents.

* * * * *

Nos. 6 and 7 are two Liſts, one of a lot of old, and the other of a lot of young, male and female Negroes, ſent hither by Vice Director

Beck in the Ship *New Netherland Indian.* Annexed thereto is a return of the conditions and prices at which they were fold here.

✻ ✻ ✻ ✻ ✻

Refolution of the Director and Council of New Netherland.

Monday, 7th November, 1661.

IN COUNCIL. Prefent—
 Director General *Petrus Stuyvefant,*
 Honble *Nicafius de Sille,*
 Johan de Decker.

RESOLVED, to fell four more of the 7 Negroes, held over laft year, to the higheft bidder at public auction on the following Conditions:

The Buyers fhall be empowered to ufe the purchafed Negroes as

Aa

Bond Slaves, alfo to refell them to others either within or beyond this Province, provided that whomfoever will remove or tranfport them beyond this Province, fhall pay for each Negro a duty of Two Beavers.

Payment fhall be made down at lateft within fix weeks from date hereof in Wheat or Rye.

The Wheat at 3 Guilders, and the Rye at 2½ Gl. the Skepel.

The Negroes fhall be delivered to the Purchafers at the time of payment and not before.

The Purchafers fhall be bound to give fufficient fecurity.

Contract for a Cargo of Slaves for New Netherland.

THIS day the Meff[rs] *Abraham Wilmerdonx* and *Jacob Pergens*, both Directors of the Weſt India Company at the Chamber here, being ſpecially authorized thereto by their Aſſociates, on the one part, and *Hendrick Roeters*, old ſchepen, *Johan Tayſpil* and *Anthony Caſteleyn*, Commiſſaries and Directors of this City's Colonie in *New Netherland*, by their Aſſociates thereunto ſpecially delegated, on the other part, agree and contract, that the abovenamed Directors intending to purchaſe a parcel of Slaves at *Angola*, and to convey them to *New Netherland*, ſhall admit the aforeſaid Commiſſioners and Directors to participate with them in the coſts and riſk of the Trade of the aforeſaid Slaves, for one fourth, in all reſpects the ſame as the Company, and that accordingly the abovenamed Directors and Commiſſioners ſhall alſo pay their portion in the moneys which are advanced to the Skipper of the *Gideon*, and the aforefaid Directors (of the Weft India Company) fhall with all poffible fpeed difpatch the Ship *Gideon*, chartered for that purpofe by their Honors, according to the Charter Party, and let it purfue its Voyage accordingly; that the abovenamed Directors fhall have the exclufive management of the aforefaid Trade and raife on bottomry the moneys required therefor, in the manner ufual with the Company, and after the Voyage is completed, account for and fettle with the abovenamed Directors and Commiffaries for every thing; and that the aforefaid Commiffioners fhall give orders that their Officers, being notified of the arrival of the aforefaid Slaves at the *Manhattans*, fhall repair thither to receive the aforefaid fourth of the faid Negroes by blind lot, and give receipt therefor; that, further, the aforeſaid Commiſſioners, as ſoon as the receipt ſhall be produced here, ſhall pay to the Company *Ten* Carolus Guilders, over and above their ſhare as above in the Trade, after delivery for each merchantable Slave from 15 to 36 years, being reckoned head for head as merchantable, and above 36 and from 15 to 8 years downwards, three for two, and from 8 years down, 2 for one, ſucklings following the mother. All under expreſs condition, that the abovenamed Directors and Commiſſioners muſt retain the aforeſaid Slaves in their Colonie without allowing them to be ſold to any other Nation outſide the Colonie, or ſuffering them to be either directly or indirectly removed or ſold elſewhere. All upon the penalty of 300 Florins for each Slave who shall be removed, or such higher penalty as is provided or may hereafter be provided in the Ordinances already enacted, or that shall hereafter be enacted therefor in *New Netherland.*

Directors at Amsterdam to Director STUYVESANT.

Amsterdam, 20*th January,* 1664.

* * * * *

IN our last which we enclose, you were informed that we contracted with *Symon Gilde,* Skipper of the Ship *Gideon,* to export a goodly number of Slaves from *Loango* on the Coast of *Africa,* and to convey them by way of *Curaçao* to *New Netherland;* also that this City is a partner therein for one fourth part, as may be more fully seen by the Copies hereunto annexed.

As the Slaves are intended solely to promote Agriculture, which is the only means of making the State prosperous, so is it our express order, that the aforesaid Slaves shall be sold there only to our Inhabitants on the express condition, that they shall not be exported out of our district, but specially retained therein, to be employed in the cultivation of the soil, so that the great expense which we have incurred may not be fruitless, but that we may, in due course of time, reap the fruits which we promise ourselves therefrom. The aforesaid Ship with about 300 Slaves may, according to our calculation, arrive yonder in the month of June or July next.

As your Honor will be greatly relieved by this supply, you will therefore use every effort that one third part at least of the proceeds shall be forwarded hither in Beaver, in order that we may be enabled to pay the freight, or the greatest part thereof at farthest, on the arrival of the aforesaid Ship here, which we are bound to do by contract. Otherwise, we shall lose all ambition to continue such transmission of Slaves. This we commend to your Honor's special consideration.

Director Stuyvesant *to Vice Director* Beck.

Amsterdam in *New Netherland,*
7 *May,* 1664.

* * * * *

MESS^{rs} the Directors, and the Commissioners of the Colonie on the *South River,* have entered into a contract with *Simon Cornelijfen Gilde*, Skipper of the *Gideon*, to tranfport hither a lot of Negroes for Agricultural purpofes. Thefe Negroes will, we hope, have arrived before this Letter reaches your Honor, or, at leaft, be embarked after its receipt. We fhall therefore recommend that, being properly provided, they may be difpatched hither as fpeedily as poffible. If it happen that *Simon Gilde* fhould arrive with the Negroes at the Ifland of *Curaçao* a month later than the Charter Party provides, fay, the middle of Auguft, the firft inftalment might reach here before or by the middle of September from *Curaçao*, and the remainder by the middle of October. In that event a fair price might be realized for them.

Conditions and Terms on which the Director General and Council of New Netherland propoſe to ſell to the higheſt bidder a lot of Negroes and Negreſſes. 29 May, 1664.

THE Buyers ſhall immediately take poſſeſſion of their purchaſed Negroes, and may uſe them as Bond Slaves, and alſo ſell them to others.

But whereas, the meaning of the Directors is, to promote and advance the Population and Agriculture of this Province more and more, the purchaſed Negroes or Negreſſes ſhall not be ſold, carried away or tranſported beyond this Province. Whoſo acts contrary hereunto, ſhall forfeit for each Negro or Negrefs, *One hundred* Guilders, Beaver value.

Payment fhall be made, one fourth part down, the remainder in *September* or *October* next, in good Beaver at *Eight* Guilders the Skin, or in Merchandize, Beaver price, or in Provifions fuch as the Honble Company may require, to be delivered here at the *Manhattans* at the following prices:

Wheat at 55 Stivers,
Peafe at 50 Stivers, } the Skepel.
Rye at 45 Stivers,

Salted Beef at 4 Stivers,
Pork at 5 Stivers, } the Pound.

The Purchafer fhall be bound to give fufficient fecurity.

On the foregoing Conditions, the following were the Purchasers:

Florins.

Jacobus Backer, - 1 Negro, for 555
       1 Negress,   305
       1 Negro,   315
          —— 1175
Dom^e Johannes Theodorus Polhemius, on Colonists' Account, one Negro for - - - - - - 440
Nicolas Verleth, on Colonists' Account,
    1 Negress,   for *fl.* 290
    1 Negro,   395
    1 Negress and Child, 360
    1 Negress,   260
          —— 1305
Johannes Verveelen,   - 1 Negro, 445
Paulus Leendertsen Vande Grift,
          1 Negro, 425
Capt. Thomas Willet, - 1 Negro, 502
Timotheus Gabry, -   - 1 Negro, 485
Mr John Laurence, -   1 Negro, 345
Jerominus Ebbingh,   - 1 Negro, 485
Isaacq Foreest, -   - 1 Negro, 545
Jacob Leyseler, -   - 1 Negro, 615
Nicolas De Meyer, -   1 Negro, 460
Daniel Terneur, -   - 1 Negro, 465
Isaac Bedlo, -   - 1 Negro, 430

Jacques Couſſeaa, -	1 Negreſs,	335
	1 ditto,	305
	1 ditto,	300
		940
William Maerſchalck,	1 Negro,	500
	1 ditto,	425
		925
Govert Loocquermans, -	1 Negro,	305
Egbert Myndertſen, -	1 Negro,	562
Adriaen Vincent,	- 1 Negreſs,	255
Carel van Brugge, -	1 Negreſs,	300
	1 Negro,	600
		900

Total Florins, 12009

Director STUYVESANT *to the Directors at Amſterdam.*

* * * * *

THIS day fortnight arrived here your Honors' Veſſel, the *Sparrow,* with *Forty* head of Slaves, ſent to us by Vice Director *Beck* to procure Proviſions and all ſorts of

Timber work, fix Ox Carts and a new Rofmill. * * *

The Negroes and Negreffes have all arrived fafely and in health, but were, on an average, pretty old, and as the Skipper alleges, rejected by the Spaniards. The product of the greater part appears by the accompanying account of the public Vendue. They would have brought more, had they not been fo old. *Five* of the Negro Women, who were, in our opinion, unfaleable, have been kept back and remain unfold. In like manner, *Six* Negroes alfo, to help to cut the required Timber and to perform fome other neceffary work for the Honorable Company.

10 *June*, 1664.

Directors at Amsterdam to Director STUYVESANT.

Amsterdam, 24 *June*, 1664.

Honorable, Prudent, Valiant, Beloved, Faithful.

WE have heretofore advised you of our intention to let the Ship *Gideon* go from *Curaçao* to the *Manhattans* with her Slaves. Having since then, and now for the first time, remarked the hostile and treacherous designs manifested by the English towards the Company's rightful Conquests on the Coast of *Africa*, where they have already mastered *Cape Verd* and taken 3 (*a*: 4 of the Company's Ships or Yachts, we have come to a different determination. As your Honor also will not be left unmolefted by them, for we underftand that they have likewife fent 3 Ships with Men thither to the afliftance of their Nation, and as the aforefaid Ship with Slaves might hereby be brought into difficulty, we have thought proper to fend her firft to the *South River*, to learn there from the City's Director how matters ftand at the *Manhattans*. On learning the arrival of this Ship there, your Honor muft immediately commiffion fome one to go thither, to be prefent at the allotment of the Negroes, and to repair to the *Manhattans* with the fhare, or ¾th the part that is to fall to the Company; with this underftanding, however, that if the abovenamed Ship had not brought thither above 200 head, there fhall be left to the City at leaft 60 head, as we find ourfelves under obligation to accommodate them with that number.

Herewith,
Honorable, Prudent, Valiant, Beloved, Faithful,
Commending you to God's merciful Protection, we Remain,
Your Good Friends,
The Directors of the Incorporated Weſt India Company, Chamber at *Amſterdam*,

J. BONTEMANTEL,
DAVID VAN BAERLE.

Vice Director BECK *to the Directors and Council of New Netherland.*

Curaçao in *Fort Amfterdam,* the 21. *July,* Año 1664.

Honorable, Valiant, Wife, Prudent and right Difcreet Gentlemen.

Gentlemen,

MY laſt to your Honors was dated 28 April, by the Company's Ship *Mufch*, which I not only hope has arrived in your parts long before your receipt of this, but ardently defire to fee her return here every day.

Since then a handfome Genoefe (*genuees*) Ship, named the *Sta Cruz*, arrived here from *Cartagena*, with One hundred and *fixty thoufand* pieces of Eight in Specie, to be all invefted in Slaves through the Factors refiding here on behalf of the Genoefe Company, who, however up to this time have delayed doing any thing, by advice and order of their Principals, in the expectation that they will have concluded a new Contract with the Company, and that more Slaves may arrive here, fo as to inveft the entire Capital which they have brought for that purpofe in their aforefaid Ship, in Slaves and to carry them away at once.

On the 8th inftant, arrived here by way of *Guinea, Angola,* and *Cayenne,* the Ship *Gideon,* the bearer hereof, *Simon Corneliffen Gilde,* Skipper, with over *Three hundred* Slaves. I was in hopes by means of thefe and the fupply of Slaves already here, to have enough to be able on the Advice and Order of the Company, to accommodate the aforefaid

Factors for their abovementioned Specie, as then was their intent; for they said, in case no seasonable advice or order was received from their Principals and the Company, that they would then contract with me for as many Slaves as were here at present, and might happen to arrive, to be paid for on delivery, in order to dispatch their aforesaid Ship, which was lying here at great expense. So they were expecting that they could have availed themselves on this occasion, for their Vessel, of the Slaves brought hither by the aforesaid Ship *Gideon*, when the abovementioned Skipper *Simon Corneliffen Gilde* brought me such ample Order and Instructions to the contrary, that I could not dare to change them, as your Honors will please to observe by the annexed Copies. Pursuant to said Orders

I am fending to your Honors herewith, by the aforefaid Ship and Skipper the number of Slaves to be feen in the accompanying Invoice and Bill of Lading to which, for brevity's fake, I refer.

And fince now, in the firft place, no more Slaves are to be expected here, the aforefaid Factors will have to content themfelves with the Slaves which have been previoufly brought hither on the Company's account; and as many of the Slaves brought here by the faid Ship *Gideon* are infected with Scurvy, I have therefore retained the greater number of thefe here and embarked others in their place from among thofe brought in previous Ships. When thofe are cured of the Scurvy, they can be delivered, in the place of the others, to the aforefaid Factors.   *   *   *   *   *

Bill of Lading for Three Hundred Negroes sent to the Manhattans.

I, UNDERWRITTEN *Simon Corneliffe Gilde*, Skipper under God of my Ship, named the *Gideon*, now lying in the Harbor of *Curaçao*, ready to fail with the firſt fair wind (which God ſhall vouchſafe) for the *Manhatans* in *New Netherland* acknowledge to have received between the Decks of my aforeſaid Ship, the number of *Three hundred* Slaves, conſiſting of *One hundred* and *ſixty* Men and *One hundred* and *forty* Women, all merchantable; which Slaves I promiſe to deliver (if God grant me a proſperous Voyage), with my aforeſaid Ship at the ſaid *Manhatans* to the

Honble Director General *Petrus Stuyvefant* or his Order, on payment of my freight for the aforefaid Slaves, as agreed upon and conditioned by the Charter Party, and for the performance of what precedes, I pledge myfelf and all my Property and my aforefaid Ship with all its Appurtenances. In witnefs of the truth I have figned three Invoices, all of the fame tenor, the one being fulfilled, the others are void. Written at *Curaçao*, the 21ft *July*, Año 1664. (Signed)

SYMON CORNELISSEN GILDE.

Director Stuyvesant *to Vice Director* Beck.

Honorable, Prudent, Wife, and very Difcreet Sir.

OUR laft Letter to you was by the Ship *The White Horfeman*, Skipper *Hendrick Janfen Stuyvefant*, dated the 7th May laft.   *   *   *

Since then, viz., on the 24th May, arrived here in fafety, God be praifed, the Company's Ship *Sparrow*, Skipper *Jan Peterfen Groot* of *Dockum*, by whom I received your Honor's Letter of the 28th of April, to which the following will ferve as an anfwer.

The Slaves and Merchandize arrived fafely according to Invoice and Bill of Lading.   *   *   *

I have fold the Negroes that have been fent, at Public auction to the higheſt bidder, for Proviſions, with the exception of *Six* of the Men, who are employed in the Company's ſervice on the Works of the Fort, and *Five* Negro Women who, on account of their advanced Age, could not find a Purchaſer, except at a very low figure. The remainder have been ſold at prices mentioned in the annexed Copy of the Conditions of the Sale; being, in our opinion, a tolerably fair price for ſuch a lot. Had they been better, there is not a doubt but they would have produced a much larger amount, as may be inferred from the price of a few who were ſold for 600 Guilders[*] and upwards.

Theſe Negroes have afforded us great relief in the purchaſe of Proviſions for the Garriſon. Otherwiſe,

[*] $240.

we should have been constrained by the low state of the Treasury, caused by the continued troubles, first with the Barbarians, and now at present with the neighboring English, to purchase Supplies by Bills of Exchange.

* * * * *

In our former dispatch, duplicate whereof we here inclose, we stated among other things, if it should come to pass that *Simon Gilde* arrived at the Island of *Curaçao*, with Negroes three weeks or a month later than intimated in the Charter Party, say the middle of August, therefore the sending of the Negroes hither should not be postponed, &c. Having reconsidered this, we have, for divers reasons, whereof one is, that the Right Honorable the Regents of the city of *Amsterdam* are interested therein one fourth part, thought it beft and moft juftifiable, not to make the flighteft alteration in the Charter Party which the Directors have concluded with *Simon Gilde*. Wherefore we requeft and recommend your Honor to regulate yourfelf by the faid Charter Party in the forwarding of the abovementioned Negroes. But as we find ourfelves burthened here by an unufually ftrong Garrifon, for the fupport of which, exclufive of the monthly pay, we require confiderable Provifions, for the purchafe whereof we are not well provided; we, on that account, have need, yea great need of a few Slaves, in order to truck them for Provifions. Yet, for reafons already given, we deem it unjuftifiable to fend for the faid Negroes, contrary to the Charter Party concluded with *Simon Gilde*.

Yet requiring a large quantity of Provifions both for this place and *Curaçao*, as we have already ftated and more fully explained, fhould an opportunity offer to purchafe any, funds would be abfolutely neceffary. Wherefore we recommend this ferioufly to your confideration; and if *Simon Gilde* arrive in feafon, to fend us as many Negroes as circumftances will permit. If Negroes be fcarce, which however we fhould prefer to have for the good and advancement of the country, according to the Honble Company's Order, fome other effects, either Money or Ofnaburghs and other coarfe Linen, or any thing elfe that is not needed for the public fervice, might be fpared and bartered for Provifions. If Negroes, your Honor will pleafe to bear in mind to have them fent off in time that they may probably arrive here before, or about All Saints, and that they be fuitably provided againſt the cold.

30 *July*, 1694.

The Council of New Netherland to the Directors at Amſterdam.

*   *   *   *   *

MEANWHILE, God be thanked, the Ship *St. Jacob* arrived here in fafety on the 13th inſtant, from the *South River*, and, two days after, the Ship *Gideon*, which failed from *Curaçao* on the 21ſt of July with 300 Slaves, 160 Men and 140 Women, whereof 9 died on the paſſage. This is a very poor lot; indeed fo poor do we believe, that we fear the moſt of them will remain on our hands, or muſt be let go at a very low figure, whereof more in our next.

Purſuant to the Contract which your Honors made with the Directors of the City's Colonie, we have delivered by lot the fourth part of the abovementioned Negro Men and Women, into the hands of Mr *Peter Alrichs*, Commiſſary of Indian Cargoes, and Councillor of the Colonie of *New Amſtel*, who has been here for ſome time for the purpoſe of purchaſing Oxen, Cows and Horſes, to the number of 200 or thereabouts. * * *

The Colonie has received by lot for its fourth part, 38 Men and 34 Women. But as there were among theſe, as well as among thoſe that fell to the Company, many above the age of 36 years, three of them muſt be counted for two. * * *

This ferves merely to advife your Honors of the arrival of the above-mentioned Negroes who, though a very poor lot, as already ftated, yet in our moft deplorable ftate, will wonderfully relieve us, fo that we and your Honors' Servants and Inhabitants, find ourfelves greatly obliged, and gratefully acknow-ledge your care in the fending of the faid Negroes. * * * *

Fort *Amfterdam* in *New Nether-land*, 17 *Auguft*, 1664.

(By Way of the *South River*, per the *Eagle*.)

Receipt for the above Negroes.

WE the underfigned Director General and Council of *New Netherland*, hereby certify and declare that the bearer hereof, *Symon Corneliffen Gilde*, Skipper, under *God*, of the Ship *Gideon*, on the day after his arrival, being the 14th of Auguſt, hath delivered here on ſhore for account of Meſſ^rs the Directors of the Incorporated Weſt India Company, Chamber at *Amſterdam*, *Two hundred* and *ninety* head of Negroes, to wit, *One hundred* and *fifty three* Men, and *One hundred* and *thirty ſeven* Women, among whom in all were found by impartial Men as ſelected according to the Charter Party, *Eighty nine* which were judged to be above *Thirty ſix* years old; of which delivery, the abovementioned Skipper, *Symon Corneliſſen Gilde*, demanding proper Receipt to ſerve him agreeably to his Charter Party, with the abovementioned Directors, we have executed for him two of the ſame tenor, one whereof being ſatisfied, the other is to be null. Done *Amſterdam* in

New Netherland, the 30 *August,* 1664.

Permit to tranfport Negroes.

THE Honble Director General informed the Council that Capt. *Thomas Willet* would accept 3 or 4 Negroes in payment of the Beavers due him by the Company, if he might tranfport them from this place to fuch other that he may think proper. Which being taken into confideration, it was, on queftion being put, Refolved to let him have 3 or 4 Negroes; becaufe from the low ftate of the Treafury, it is not well known how elfe to fatisfy him for the Provifions delivered laft year, amounting to about *Eight thoufand* Guilders; and Secretary *Van Ruyven* is deputed to inform faid *Willet* thereof, and to agree with him about the price for the beſt advantage of the Company, and if poſſible to obtain from him as much as the General hath lately had from him for two of his own Negroes. Done 30th *September*, 1664.

Vice Director BECK *to* PETER STUYVESANT.

Curaçao, in *Fort Amſterdam* the
15 *Novembr*, Año 1664.

Sir,

* * * * *

I HAVE remarked, among other things, in your Honor's acceptable Letter, the ſerious miſtake that has been committed here in the ſale of your Slaves; eſpecially of the little Children, ſince with great forethought on the part of Madam *Stuyvefant*, your Honor's fpoufe, they were prefented at the baptifmal Font. If we had had the leaft knowledge of the Fact, the miftake would not have occurred. To my grief, a great error has been committed which I fear is irreparable; for fo long an interval has elapfed, it will be very difficult to afcertain where they have been finally landed. But I fhall have inquiries made by the firft Ship that leaves here for *Carthagena* and *Porto Bello*, and if it be poffible, endeavor to get them back, even if I fhould have to give two full grown Slaves and more for them.

Vice Director Beck *to* Peter Stuyvesant.

Curaçao, 16 *April*, Año 1665.

Sir,

 ※ ※ ※ ※ ※

A SHIP, named *Miſs Catarina*, whereof *Jacob Dirckſen Willree* is Skipper, arrived here on the 14th January laſt, from *Ardra*, on the Coaſt of *Guinea*, with *One hundred* and *fifty* Slaves. She was ſent in the Service of the Company from *Amſterdam* to the *Caſtle del Mina* to Mr. *Valckenburgh* with ſome Supplies for that place, and ſucceeded very well, notwithſtanding many Engliſh Ships were off that Coaſt.

 * * * * *

Since my laſt, I have ſold here

to the Genoefe (*genueefen*) all the Slaves which had come here on the Company's account in the laft Ships and were remaining at this place (*a One hundred* and *twenty* pieces of Eight. And becaufe of thefe Englifh troubles, and principally becaufe no Slaves were expected here from the Coaft of *Guinea*, the aforefaid Genoefe have taken their departure hence with their Ship and the abovementioned purchafed Slaves, on the 23d January laft for *Carthagena*. We fhall learn betimes whether this trade fhall be renewed in *Holland* with the Company, or whether it will be purfued and continued at this place by other Spaniards.

I have, fince that, been informed that the Principals of the abovementioned Genoefe in *Spain* have contracted with the Royal Company of *England* for the delivery of Slaves, such delivery to be made at the Island of *Jamaica*, and that a large Ship belonging to the said Genoese has already arrived at *Jamaica*, to carry away the Slaves, according to the Contract concluded with the Royal Company. But inasmuch as no Slaves had reached there for the Royal Company, they were allowed to purchase as many Slaves from the English Planters and Inhabitants as they were to receive. In regard to this Contract, all Commissions of Privateers and Ships against the Spaniards in these *West Indies* are revoked, and they are forbidden to inflict any damage on the Spanish Nation by land or water; and when a rich Spanish Prize was brought by the English Privateers into *Jamaica*, they were obliged to restore her, free of costs and charges.

I doubt if this Englifh Royal Company will be able to fulfill their Contract with the Genoefe, if it be of any magnitude, in confequence of the difturbances and troubles caufed by themfelves on the Coaft of *Guinea* and the great obftruction they will encounter as long as thefe troubles continue, in their Slave Trade and in all their other Commerce, from the Privateers of *Holland* and *Zealand*, of which they have had, hitherto, no fufpicion.

* * * * *

We fee now here for the fecond time a Comet with a long fiery tail; it has been vifible here for more than two months paft. It is alfo vifible in *Europe*. What it portends is beft known only to the Chief Giver of all Good, who will mercifully turn away from us all

well deferved plagues and punifh-
ments, and make every thing tend
to the honor of his Moſt Holy
Name for the Good of His People
unto Salvation.

*　　*　　*　　*　　*

INDEX.

AFFIDAVIT of Jan van Gaelen, 14; of Jan Rykartien, 27; of Hans Marcuffen Stuyve, 35; of Adriaen Blaes, 45.
Africa, Guinea Traders refort to, vii; private Dutch Traders not allowed to go to, xv; Trade to, opened to New Netherland, xxi; Colonifts of New Netherland permitted to bring Negroes from, 103; Slaves to be taken to the Weft Indies from, 103; and to New Netherland, 104, 107; a Ship fails from Medenblick to, for Slaves, 112; Ship Eyckenboom chartered to convey Slaves to New Netherland from, 132; Limits wherein private Merchants may trade for Slaves in, 170, 173; Inhabitants of New Netherland allowed to trade to, 172; hoftile Defigns of the Englifh on the Dutch Forts in, 207.
African Company, Royal, contract to fell Slaves, 230.
Africans introduced into New Netherland, xiii.
Agriculture, the Slave Trade authorized for the Benefit of, xxvi, 107; Negroes imported into New Netherland for the Promotion of, 165, 168, 180, 185, 199.
Alrichs, Peter, Slaves delivered to, 222.

Ff

Amandaré, the firſt Slave Ship in New Netherland, xvi; came probably from Brazil, xxiv; brings Negroes to New Netherland, 99.
Amboſius, Highland of, 3, 46.
America, Virginia Traders reſort to, vii.
Amſterdam City, owns Shares in a Slave Ship, xxvi; contracts for a Cargo of Slaves, 195.
Amſterdam Chamber of the W. I. Co., informed of the Loſs of the Slaver St. John, and the Capture of her Slaves, 78; authorizes the Importation of Slaves into New Netherland, 108; directs the Seizure of a Ship belonging to Medenblick that ſailed to Africa for Slaves, 112; contracts to ſupply Slaves, 153, 160; orders a freſh Supply of Negroes to be ſent to New Netherland, 184; determined to encourage the Slave Trade, 185; trades in Slaves, 195, 198.
Angola, Blacks from, captured, ix, x, xi; Trade from Holland to, xiii; Slaves obtained at, 91; Coloniſts of New Netherland permitted to trade to, 101, 102; Slaves purchaſed at, 195.
d'Angola, Paul, xiii.
Annebo, Iſland of, 6; Proviſions for Slavers purchaſed at, 7, 47.
Arda, 2.
Arms of Amſterdam, Journal of the Slaver, 87; captured by a Pirate, 93.
Arobe, equivalent of the, 125.
Aruba, 27, 49, 58.
Aſſembly of the XIX, Reſolution of, 105.
Auction, Negroes ſold at, xii, 168, 190, 193, 202, 216.

BACKER, Jacobus, 204.
Barbadoes, a Dutch Slaver lofes fome Negroes at, xvi; a Slave Emporium, xxix.
Barley raifed in New Netherland, xviii.
Beans raifed in New Netherland, xviii.
Beaulieu, Captain, a Privateer, 84.
Beaver, Price of, 203.
Beck, Matthias, Vice Director of Curaçao, fends Sloops to take Slaves off the wrecked St. John, 8, 14, 41, 49; iffues a Proclamation for the Arreft of Pirates, 69; Letters of, 78, 83; authorized to feize a Medenblick Slaver, 112; fupplies Spaniards with Slaves, 160; fends Negroes to New Netherland, 181, 205; ordered to fend a frefh Supply of Negroes to New Netherland, 182.
Bedlo, Ifaac, 204.
Beef, falt, Price of, 203.
Bills of Lading for Negroes, 140, 176, 181, 214.
Black Eagle, Ship, fails for New Netherland, 106.
Blacks, the Weft India Company promife to fupply New Netherland with, xiv.
Blaes, Adriaen, Skipper of the Slaver St. John, 5, 17; Affidavit of, 45.
Bloody Flux, Slaves fuffering from, 4; Surgeon De Lanoy dies of the, 6.
Bonaire, 15, 48, 50.
Bontemantel, J., Director of the Weft India Company, 209.
Brafil, Number of Slaves brought into, viii; Effect of the Conqueft of, on the Slave Trade, xi, xii; private Dutch Veffels not allowed to trade to, xv; Trade opened between New Netherland and,

xix; Slaves to be brought from, xx; Colonifts of New Netherland permitted to trade to, 101; Negroes may be exported from, 106.
Bread, Want of, on board the Slaver St. John, 8.
Brommert, Captain, commands an Englifh Privateer, 93.
Bruyn, Frans, 140; purchafes Slaves for Director Stuyvefant, 144.

CABO de Loop de Confalvo, 5; Slaver procures Wood and Water at, 6, 47.
Caerloff, Hendrick, builds a Fort for the Swedes at Cape Corfe, 174.
Calabari, a Slave Mart, 45, 46.
Cape Corfe, the Swedes build a Fort at, 174.
Cape Verde, Negroes from, fold at Curaçao, 154; Slaves received at Curaçao from, 155; the Englifh capture, 207.
Caraccas, Operations of Pieterfen the Privateer at, 21, 36, 37, 56, 57; Trade between Curaçao and, 113, 115, 117, 118.
Carthagena, a Ship arrives for Slaves at Curaçao from, 210; Slaves fent from Curaçao to, 229.
Cafteleyn, Anthony, 195.
Caftle Frigate, Jan Pieterfen, a Dane, commands the Privateer, 18, 30, 40, 53, 69.
Cayman Iflands, Pirates capture a Dutch Ship at the, 92.
Charter of a Ship for a Voyage to Africa and New Netherland, 132.
Children, Number of, who died on board the Slaver St. John, 12.

Claeffen, Peter, cooper, Death of, 4; at Rio Cammerones, 6.
Colding, Situation of, 31.
Colonies, Englifh, the Dutch introduce Slaves into the, vi; to be fupplied with Slaves by the Dutch, 184.
Comet, a, vifible at Curaçao and in Europe, 231.
Conditions on which Negroes are to be fold by Auction at New Amfterdam, 193, 202.
Congo, Simon, xiii.
Contract made with the Directors at Amfterdam for Slaves, 153, 160; to import Slaves into New Netherland, Draft of a, 169; for a Cargo of Slaves for New Netherland, 194.
Copper, brought from the Spanifh Main, 118.
Cormantyn, the Englifh build a Fort at, 174.
Couffeau, Jacques, 205.
Couwenhoven, Peter, 175.
Cuba, Propofal to run Negroes into, 120; not feafible, 132.
Curaçao, Effect of the Capture of, on the Slave Trade, xi, xii; a Slave Emporium, xxix; Slaver St. John fails for, 8; Crew of the St. John arrive at, 13; Slaves fent from Africa to, 91; a Ship fent from Medenblick to convey Slaves to, 112; Trade between the Spanifh Main and, 113, 154; Spaniards invited to trade at, 116, 117; the Slave Trade at, 121, 125, 126, 127; Slaves fent to New Netherland from, 140; Slaves brought from Guinea to, 143; weak State of, 157; Negroes fent to New Netherland from, 177, 178; a Ship from Carthagena arrives at, for Slaves, 210;

Slaves arrive at New Amsterdam from, 221; sent to Carthagena from, 229; a Comet visible at, 231 (See *Slave Trade*).

DAVID'S Island, 21, 24, 30, 57.
Decker, Johan, de, 189, 193.
De Groot, Arent, builds a Fort at Cormantyn, 174.
De Laet, Johannis, his Opinion of Blacks, ix.
De Lanoy, Surgeon Martin, dies, 6.
Delaware (See *South River*).
Douwneman, Robert, a Pirate, captures a Dutch Ship and Cargo, 92.
Dutch, the original Introducers of Slaves into the North American Colonies, vi; did not place much Value on the Slave Trade at first, xi; Number of Slaves captured from the Spaniards by the, xii; additional Papers relative to the Slave Trade under the, 99; the chief Supporters of the Slave Trade, 104.
Duty on Negroes, 171, 185, 194.

EBBINGH, Jeronimus, 204.
Edsal, Samuel, sends a crazy Negro to Virginia to be sold, 182.
Elephants' Teeth brought from Africa, 31, 40, 65.
Elizabeth's River, Virginia, 95.
Elmina, 1; bad Provisions supplied at, 5; Johan Valckenburgh Director at, 45; Slaver Arms of Amsterdam sails from, 90.
English, the, well supplied in America with Provisions, xix; Slaves to be exported by the Dutch to

(239)

the, xxv; have a Fort at Cormantyn, 174; Capture Cape Verd, 207.
Eyckenboom, Jan Janſen, of Hoorn, 133; conveys Negroes to New Netherland, 176.
Eyckenboom, Ship, chartered to carry Slaves from Africa to New Netherland, 132; arrives at New Amſterdam with Horſes and Negroes, 178.

FAITH, the Ship, 192.
Fayal, Negroes ſent to, x.
Florida, no private Dutch Veſſel allowed to trade North of, xv.
Foreeſt, Iſaac, 204.
Foſcom, Mr., 89; his Bark arrives at New Amſterdam from Virginia, 95.
Franciſco, John, xiii.
Frederick, Prince, Declaration of one of the Magiſtrates of Amſterdam to, 104.
Freedoms to Patroons, encourage Agriculture in New Netherland, xviii.
Friar Francis, trades with the Dutch at Curaçao, 124, 125, 126.
Froon, Johan, Commiſſary on board the St. John, 45.

GABRIE, Thimotheus, 175, 204.
Genoeſe, the, trade for Slaves at Curaçao, 210, 211, 229.
Gey, Captain, commands an Engliſh Privateer, 93.
Gideon, Ship, xxiv, 147; carries Slaves to Curaçao, 155; ſent to Africa for Slaves, 156, 198, 201, 207; arrives at Curaçao, 211; arrives at Manhattans with 300 Slaves, 221.

Gilde, Symon C., 122; fells Negroes at Curaçao, 126; contracts to convey Slaves from Africa to New Netherland, 198, 201; commands Ship Gideon, 147, 149; contracts to convey 300 Slaves to the Manhatans, 214; Receipt for them to, 223.
Gilded Eagle, Ship, 192.
Groot, Jan Pieterfen, Skipper of the Ship Sparrow, 141; brings Slaves to the Manhattans, 216; (See *Pieterfen*).
Guinea, Slaves brought by the Dutch from, vii, xxiv, 28, 35, 79; a Cargo of Negroes arrives in New Netherland from, 110, 179; Slaves taken to Curaçao from, 147; Ship Gideon arrives with Slaves from, 211, 228.

HACK, Nicolas, Secretary of Curaçao, 27, 34, 44, 68, 162.
Havana, Vice Director Beck writes to the Governor of, 152.
Heermans, Auguftine, 142, 146.
Hifpaniola, Spanifh Veffels captured off, x.
Holland, Courfe of Trade between Africa and, xiii.
Horfes and Negroes arrive at New Netherland from Curaçao, 178; Lofs fuftained in New Netherland by the Sale of, 187.

INFORMATION refpecting the Capture of the Slaves on board the St. John, 14.
Introduction of Slavery into New Netherland, xiii.

JACQUES (See *Van Cuelen*).
Jamaica, Sea Rovers arrive at, 85; Slaves to be furnifhed at, 230.
Janfen, Skipper Dirck, carries Negroes to New Netherland, 181.
Janfen, Skipper Ewout, 153.
Jews, in purchafing Slaves, Chriftians ought to be preferred to unbelieving, 165.
Journal of the Slaver St. John, 1; of the Slaver Arms of Amfterdam, 87.

KING Solomon, Ship, 78; arrives at Curaçao with Slaves, 143.
Kregier, Martin, 175.

LA Garce, Privateer, vifits New Amfterdam, xxiii.
La Montagne, Mr., 110.
Laurence, John, 204.
Leeuw, Peter de, 26, 34, 44, 68.
Letters of Vice Director Beck to the Weft India Company, 78, 113, 124, 147; to Director Stuyvefant, 83; of the Directors at Amfterdam to Director Stuyvefant, 99, 101, 103, 106, 167, 183, 198, 207.
Leyfeler, Jacob, 204.
Limits wherein private Perfons may trade for Slaves in Africa, 170, 173.
Lift of Slaves who died on the Paffage from Africa to Curaçao, 10.
Loando, reduced by the Dutch, xii; Effect of the

Gg

Reduction, xv; a Slave Mart, 91; Slaves carried to New Netherland from, 198.
Loocquermans, Govert, 175, 205.
Lord, Richard, purchafes a Negro, 100.
Lubbertfen, Frederick, fells a Negro to Richard Lord, 100.
Lucaffen, Theunis, 26.

MAERSCHALCK, William, 205.
Man, Edward, Director of the Weft India Company, 132, 186.
Manhattan, the firft Slaves brought to, xiii; Inhabitants of, permitted to bring Negroes from Africa, 102; Slaves to be brought from Africa to, 196, 207; Inftructions regarding Slaves for, 208; three hundred Slaves fent to, 214.
Maria of London, a Pirate, commanded by Capt. Douwneman, 92; burnt, 94.
Matthias, Henricus, contracts to deliver Negroes at Curaçao, 121, 122.
Medenblick, a Ship fails to Africa from, for Slaves, 112.
Men, Number of, who died on board the Slaver St. John, 12.
Merchants of New Amfterdam remonftrate againft the Reftrictions on the Slave Trade, 171.
Meyer, Nicolas de, 204.
Michielfen van Hulft, Martin, 62.
Mifs Catarina, Ship, brings Slaves from Guinea to Curaçao, 228.
Momma, Guillaume, contracts to fupply Slaves, 153, 155, 161.

Montferrat, 94.
Myndertfen, Egbert, 205.

NANCIMON (Va.), 95.
Negroes, firft introduced into the Colonies, vii; little valued by the Dutch, ix, x, xi; Number of, captured by the Dutch, xii; fold for Pork and Peas, xvi; brought by Privateers into New Amfterdam, xxiii; fome lufty, about to be fent to Director Stuyvefant, 86; two killed, 93; the Directors at Amfterdam promife to fupply New Netherland with more, 99; Bill of Sale of a, 100; New Netherland permitted to fend to Africa for, 102, 103; taken as Prizes, may be exported from Brazil, 105; Duties on, 106; Spaniards invited to Curaçao to purchafe, 116, 119; to be run into Cuba, 120; Trade at Curaçao in, 121, 122; Price of, 123, 125, 126, 130, 143, 145, 146, 155, 161, 162, 164, 188, 204, 205, 217, 229; how to be run into the Spanifh Main, 128; Royalty in the Spanifh Colonies on, *ibid.*; Bill of Lading for, 140, 176, 181, 214; Trade in, referved by the Weft India Company, 143; ordered to be fent to New Netherland, 145; a fine Lot of, loft, 148; fold at Curaçao to Spaniards, 154; Chriftians ought to be preferred to Spaniards and Jews in purchafing, 165; for New Netherland ought to be ftout Fellows, 166; to be employed in the War againft the Indians, *ib.*; to be fold at public Auction in New Amfterdam, 168; Duty on, 171; from Curaçao arrive at New Amfterdam, 177, 178, 180; a crazy, exported to Vir-

ginia, 182; a frefh Supply of, ordered to New
Netherland, 182; Duty on exported, 185; fold
at Auction, 190, 193, 202, 216; and held as
Bond Slaves, 194; imported from Africa into
New Netherland, 201, 216; Receipt for, 223;
Thomas Willet permitted to export, 225; (See
Slaves).
New Amftel, Slaves fent to, 222.
New Amftel, Galiot, commanded by Auguftine
Heermans, 142.
New Amfterdam, Negroes brought to, xiv, xvi;
Privateers bring Slaves into, xxii, xxiii; Slaves
brought from Guinea to, xxiv; owns Slaves, xxvi;
a Veffel from Virginia arrives at, 95, Remon-
ftrance of Merchants of, againft Reftrictions on
the Slave Trade, 171; Horfes and Negroes arrive
at, 178; Negroes to be fold by Auction at, 189,
193, 202; (See *Manhattan*).
New France, private Dutch Veffels not allowed to
trade to, xv.
New Jerfey, Slavery firft noted in, xv.
New Netherland, Slavery not greatly encouraged at
firft in, xi; Hiftory of the Introduction of Slavery
into, xiii; private Dutch Veffels not allowed to
trade to, xv; firft Slave Ship arrives in, xvi; the
Slave Trade to be revived by Means of, xviii;
Products of, xviii; Trade to Brazil opened to,
xix; Slaves to be carried from Brazil to, xx;
Trade to Africa opened to, xxi; when Slaves
began to be regularly imported into, xxii; Weft
India Company refolve that Slaves fhall be kept in,
xxv; never engaged in the African Slave Trade,

xxvi; Cornelis van Tienhoven, Secretary of, 100; Trade to Brazil and Africa opened to, 101; permitted to bring Negroes from Africa, 102; Cargo of Slaves to be taken to, 104, 107, 108; and arrives at, 109; Slaves exported to Virginia from, 111; Ship chartered to convey Slaves from Africa to, 132; Slaves sent from Curaçao to, 140; what Sort of Negroes are desirable for, 166; Draft of a Contract to import Slaves into, 169; Slave Trade opened to the Inhabitants of, 172; Negroes sent from Curaçao to, 177, 178, 181; a fresh Supply of Negroes ordered to be sent to, 184; Contract for a Cargo of Slaves for, 194, 198.
New Netherland Indian, Ship, conveys Negroes to New Netherland, 181.
New Spain, Trade between Curaçao and, 159.
Nuchteren, Jan Gerritsen, Skipper of the Arms of Amsterdam, Death of, 90.

ORDINANCE imposing a Duty on Slaves exported from New Netherland, 109.
Ostrich, Ship, Hides and Tobacco sent from Curaçao to Holland by the, 125.

PADRE, a Spanish, purchases Negroes and Merchandize at Curaçao, 124, 125, 126.
Patacoon, Value of a, 145.
Patroons, Blacks promised to, xiv; undertake Agriculture in New Netherland, xviii.
Pease, raised in New Netherland, xviii; Price of, 203.
Pergens, Jacob, 194.
Permit to export Negroes, 225.

Pernambuco, the Reduction of, the great Stimulant to the Dutch Slave Trade, xi.
Pickled Herring, a Privateer, vifits New Netherland, 84.
Pieterfen, Hector, contracts to fupply Slaves, 153, 155, 161.
Pieterfen, Jacob, joins the Privateers, 43, 60, 73.
Pieterfen, Jan, a Privateer, captures a Dutch Sloop, 15; commands the Caftle Frigate, 18; Operations of, at Caraccas, 21; feizes Negroes belonging to the Weft India Company, 24, 30, 53, 61; Proclamation for the Arreft of, 69; denounced as a Pirate, 72.
Pieterfen, Jan, Skipper of the Ship Sphera Mundi, conveys Slaves to New Netherland, 140, 142; (See *Groot*).
Pirate, Proclamation for the Arreft of Jan Pieterfen, a, 69.
Pocahontas, vi.
Polhemus, Domine, 204.
Population of New Netherland, the Slave Trade tends to increafe the, 108.
Pork, Price of, 203.
Porto Bello, Slaves fupplied from Curaçao to, 155, 159.
Porto Cabelho, 118.
Porto Velo, chief Place of Trade on the Spanifh Main, 128; propofed Trade in Negroes at, 129.
Portuguefe, Anthony, xiii.
Price of Negroes, xi, xii, 123, 125, 126, 130, 143, 145, 146, 155, 161, 162, 164, 188, 204, 205, 217, 224.

Price of Wheat, Peafe and Rye, 203.
Privateer, a, brings Slaves into New Amfterdam, xxii; captures Veffels and Slaves belonging to the Dutch, 9, 15, 24, 30, 35, 51, 53; French and Englifh vifit Curaçao, 157; (See *Pieterfen*).
Proclamation for the Capture of Jan Pieterfen, a Rover, 69.

RAINS, heavy, in Africa, 4.
Receipt of a Spanifh Trader for Slaves, 160.
Remonftrance againft the Reftrictions prefcribed to private Parties engaged in the Slave Trade, 171.
Refolution of the Affembly of the XIX, 105; of the Amfterdam Chamber, 108; of the Director and Council of New Netherland, permitting Negroes to be taken to Virginia, 111; to fell Negroes at public Auction, 189, 193.
Ridder, Paulus Heyn, Pilot of the Slaver Arms of Amfterdam, Affidavit of, 89.
Rio Cammerones, 4, 46; Peter Claeffen dies at, 6.
Rio Reael, 1, 2; Slaves purchafed at, 3, 45.
Rocus, Slaver St. John loft on the Rifts of, 8, 13, 14.
Roeters, Hendrick, Schepen of Amfterdam, 195.
Rolfe, John, vi.
Rombouts, Johan, 120.
Roofa, Gyfbert, 34, 44, 68; authorized to recover a Ship captured by Pirates, and taken into Havana, 152.
Rovers, a Veffel fent in Purfuit of, 81; arrive at Jamaica, 85; Vice Director Beck unfuccefsful in his Efforts to overtake the, 148; arrefted at Havana, 152; (See *Privateer*).

Royal African Company, contract to deliver Slaves at Jamaica, 230.
Royalty in the Spanish Colonies on Negroes, 128.
Rudolphus, Pieter, 175.
Ryckartfen, Jan, Skipper of the Young Brindled Cow, 22, 50, 58, 59, 61; Affidavit of, in regard to a Privateer feizing Slaves, &c., belonging to the Dutch, 27.
Rye, produced in New Netherland, xviii; Price of, 203.

STA Cruz, a Genoefe Ship, arrives at Curaçao for Slaves, 210.
Sta. Martha, a Spanish Veffel taken off, x.
St. Catharine, a Spanish Ship, trades at Curaçao, 157.
St. Jago de Cuba, the Dutch Trade to, 152.
St. John, Slaver, Journal of, 1; Wreck of the, 8, 13, 48; Information refpecting the Capture of the Slaves on board the, 14; her lofs announced to the Directors at Amfterdam, 147.
Schaeff, Henrick, N. P., 132.
Scharburgh, Edward, carries Slaves to Virginia from New Netherland, 111.
Scurvy, Slaves on the Paffage from Guinea affected with, 213.
Ships, Englifh, capture a Dutch Slaver, 92.
Sille, Nicafius de, 110, 189, 193.
Slaver, St. John, Journal of, 1; Wreck of, 8, 48; Arms of Amfterdam, Journal of, 87; captured by a Pirate, 93.
Slavery, Hiftory of the Introduction into New

Netherland of, xiii; in New Jerfey, xv; Benefits expected to be derived from, xx, xxi.

Slaves, firft Introduction into the American Colonies of, vi; the Number of, brought into Brazil in four Years, viii; Prices of, in Brazil, xi; the firft brought to New Netherland, xiii; to be brought to New Netherland from Brazil, xx; Benefit to be derived from, xxi; when regularly imported into New Netherland, xxii; to be kept in New Netherland, and fupplied to the Englifh, xxv; Dutch trade in Africa for, 1, *et feq.*; Number of on board St. John, 5; Lift of thofe who died on the Paffage, 10; a, jumps overboard the Slaver St. John, 11; Information refpecting the Capture of the, on board the St. John, 14; Number of, captured by a Privateer, 31, 40, 65; fuffer great Mifery, and die on the Paffage for Want of Food, 47, 79; obtained at Loango, 91; to be conveyed to the Weft Indies from Africa, 103; and to New Netherland, 104, 107: Duty on exported, 109; imported at New Amfterdam from Africa, carried thence without any Benefit to the Country, 110; exported from New Netherland to Virginia, 111; a Ship fails from Medenblick for, 112; brought from Guinea to Curaçao, 143; fent to New Netherland, 144; Receipt of a Spanifh Trader for, 160; Draft of a Contract to import into New Netherland, 169; Inhabitants of New Netherland permitted to import, 172; ordered to be exported to the Englifh Colonies, 184; Prices of, in New Netherland, 188, 197 (fee *Prices*); Contract for a Cargo of, to be delivered in New Netherland, 194, 198; arrive at New Amfterdam from Curaçao, 205, 216; Ship Gideon brings 300 from Guinea, 211; affected with Scurvy, 213; arrive at New Amfterdam, 221, 224; (See *Negroes*).

Slave Ship, the firft in New Netherland, xvi.

Slave Trade, Courfe of the Dutch, xiii; lies dormant, xvii; New Netherland never directly engaged in the African, xxvi; Horrors of the, xxviii; additional Papers relative to the Dutch, 99; the Dutch the chief Supporters of the, 104; at Curaçao, 121, 125, 126, 127, 129, 153, 154, 159, 210; the only Bait to allure the Spaniards to trade with the Dutch, 151; open to private Merchants, 167; Limits prefcribed to private Parties engaged in the, 170, 173; beneficial to Agriculture and Commerce, 185; to be encouraged, 186; the Amfterdam Directors engage in, 195, 198.

Sorilho, Capt. Pedro, 153.

Soutberg, Ship, captures a Cargo of Slaves, xi.

South River, Slaves purchafed in Africa for the, 200.

Spain, the Dutch Weft India Company commence Hoftilities againft, viii.

Spaniards invited to trade at Curaçao, 116, 118; propofe to purchafe Negroes there, 122; Slaves fold at Curaçao to, 143; purchafe Negroes at Curaçao, 153, 154; Receipt of, for Slaves, 160; Ceffation of Hoftilities againft the, 230.

Spanifh Main, Royalty on Negroes at the, 128.

Sparrow, Ship, brings Slaves to New Amfterdam, 205, 216.

Spera Mundi, Ship, 83; conveys Negroes to New Netherland, 140, 142, 162.
Steendam, Jacob, 175.
Steenwyck, Cornelius, 175.
Stevenfen, Oloff, 175.
Strycker, Jacob, 175.
Stuyve, Skipper Hans Marcuffen, 14, 20, 23, 29, 49; his Veffel taken by a Privateer, 32; his Affidavit, 35.
Stuyvefant, Skipper Hendrick Janfen, 216.
Stuyvefant, Director Peter, informed of the Lofs of the Slaver St. John, 84; Vice Director Beck promifes him fome lufty Negroes, 86; Letters of the Amfterdam Directors to, 99, 101, 103, 106, 167, 183, 198, 207; Negroes purchafed for, 140, 144; acknowledges Receipt of Negroes, 163; inftructed to fell Negroes at public Auction, 168; three hundred Slaves configned to, 215; fends Slaves to Curaçao to be fold, 226.
Stuyvefant, Mrs., baptized Negro Children belonging to, fent to Curaçao and fold to Spaniards, 227.
Swedes build a Fort at Cape Corfe, 174.
Sweerts, Jan, & Co., allowed to carry a Cargo of Slaves to New Netherland, 107, 108.

TAMANDARE, Ship; (See *Amandaré*).
Tamarinds provided for Slaves, 2.
Tayfpil, Johan, 195.
Terneur, Daniel, 204.
Tobago, Ifland of, 7; Slaver St. John arrives at, 8, 47.
Trade to the Spanifh Colonies not permitted, 115;

in Negroes, reserved to the Dutch West India Company, 143; (See *Slaves*).
Troxxilla, Pedro Diez, his Receipt for Slaves, 160.

UNITED States, the Dutch introduce Slaves into the Territory, now the, vi.

VALCKENBURCH, Johan, Director at Elmina, 1, 45, 64, 91, 228.
Van Baerle, David, 209.
Van Brugge, Carel, 205.
Van Brugh, Commissary, Slaves purchased for, 144.
Van Cortlandt; (See *Stevensen*).
Van Cuelen, Leendert Jacques, Assistant Commissary on board the Slaver Arms of Amsterdam, 89.
Van Dort, Admiral, Operations of, ix.
Vande Grift, Paulus Leendertsen, 175, 204.
Vander Kemp, Dr., 104.
Vander Veer, Hendrick Jansen, 175.
Van Diemen, Claes, Death of, 2.
Van Ess, Balthazar, 120.
Van Gaelen, Jan, Affidavit of, 14; taken Prisoner, 35, 51, 55.
Van Heussen, Jasper, 1.
Van Ool, Cornelis, Price paid for Negroes by, 164.
Van Ruyven, Laurence, 144, 162.
Van Ruyven, Secretary, Slaves purchased for, 144.
Van Tienhoven, Cornelis, Secretary of New Netherland, 100.
Verleth, Nicolas, 204.
Verveelen, Johannes, 175, 204.
Vincent, Adriaen, 205.

Virginia, the Dutch introduce Slaves into, vi, vii; private Dutch Ships not allowed to trade to, xv; a Dutch Slaver carried into, xxix, 94; a Veſſel arrives at New Amſterdam from, 95; a crazy Negro ſent from New Amſterdam to, 182.

WEST India Company, Dutch, eſtabliſhed, vii; promiſes to ſupply New Netherland with Blacks, xiv; Dullneſs of the Slave Trade injurious to the, xvii; reſolves to ſupply the Colonies with Slaves, xxv; reſerves to itſelf the Trade in Negroes, 143; ſends a Cargo of Slaves to Curaçao, 228.
Weſt Indies, Dutch Merchants authorized to convey Slaves to the, 103; Hoſtilities againſt the Spaniards in the, ordered to ceaſe, 230.
Wheat, raiſed in New Netherland, xviii; Price of, 203.
Willet, Thomas, 204; permitted to export Negroes, 225.
Wilmerdonx, Abraham, Director of the Weſt India Company, 132, 194.
Willree, Jacob Dirckſen, Skipper of the Ship Catarina, brings Slaves from Guinea, 228.
Witſen, C., 186.
Wittepaert, Dirck Pieterſen, ſends a Cargo of Slaves to New Netherland, 107, 108.
Wittepaert, Ship, xxiv; ſent to Africa for Slaves for New Netherland, 107, 108; arrives in New Netherland from Guinea with Negroes, 110.
Women, Number of, who died on board the Slaver St. John, 12.
Wreck of the Slaver St. John, 8, 48.

YOUNG Brindled Cow, the Bark, sent to save the
Slaves wrecked at Rocus, 22, 50, 57.
Young Oſtrich, a Dutch Veſſel, captured by a Rover,
71.

ERRATA.

P. 73, Line 2, for *Jan* read *Jacob*.
  205, " 1, for *Couſeaa*, read *Couſeau*.
  221, " 5, for 1694, read 1664.

www.ingramcontent.com/pod-product-compliance
Lightning Source LLC
Chambersburg PA
CBHW032105220426
43664CB00008B/1146